The Politics of Expertise

CONFIGURATIONS: CRITICAL STUDIES OF WORLD POLITICS

Patrick Thaddeus Jackson, series editor

The Politics of Expertise

Competing for Authority in Global Governance

Ole Jacob Sending

University of Michigan Press
Ann Arbor

Copyright © by the University of Michigan 2015
All rights reserved

Published in the United States of America by the
University of Michigan Press
Manufactured in the United States of America
♾ Printed on acid-free paper

2018   2017   2016   2015   4   3   2   1

A CIP catalog record for this book is available from the British Library.

ISBN 978-0-472-11963-9 (hardcover : alk. paper)
ISBN 978-0-472-12125-0 (e-book)

To my family: Sofia, Kamilla, Kristian, and Siri Jo

Contents

Foreword

As academic editor for *Configurations* I am absolutely delighted that we are able to publish Ole Jacob Sending's book. Sending's book is precisely the sort of book I had in mind when initially proposing the series: it builds on the 2010 book he and Iver Neumann coauthored—*Governing the Global Polity*—and extends it in two extremely significant ways, both of which exemplify the mission of the series: to demonstrate, through concrete empirical studies, the explanatory relevance of cutting-edge social theory that privileges case-specific accounts rather than nomothetic generalizations.

Sending's first contribution is to move a significant way toward cashing in on the promise that accounts organized around particular actors' attributes and capacities has simply been unable to fulfill. The literature on advocacy networks, epistemic communities, and international bureaucracies has sought to explain policy outcomes with reference to these groups' attributes and behavioral patterns. This kind of explanation was supposed to provide an important counterweight to explanations based on power and rational self-interest. But that literature was and remains persistently unable to disaggregate the influence of the institutional position of policy experts, civil servants, and advocacy actors from their ties to traditional elements of state power; as such, that literature fails to focus on the specifically knowledge- and authority-producing activities of those groups. Claims about the significance of an epistemic community, for example, become virtually indistinguishable from claims about any other pressure group. As Sending points out, this is actually because the epistemic communities literature thinks of knowledge as something that is politically neutral as opposed to thinking of the process of knowledge-production as laded through and through with issues of struggle, recognition, and that peculiar kind of coercion that seems like a detached presentation of "the facts" but actually conceals a charged agenda. There is thus no *independent* influence of knowledgeable experts but instead an ongoing *politics of knowledge and expertise* that helps to explain how areas of international policymaking are relatively stabilized around key themes or notions. Thus, Sending's book breaks new theoretical ground as part of the overall process of exploring how international knowledge is codified into authoritative international institutional practice.

Sending's second contribution is closely related to the first: he is not simply lodging critiques of extant literature on global governance for failing to explain how and why some actors become recognized as authorities and not others. He is also demonstrating how a reconceptualization of global governance as a set of more or less autonomous and interrelated fields enables us to unpack and account for what counts as a "source" of authority in different fields and how those sources evolve over time. The politics in terms of fields and the struggles within them can help to answer questions that cannot be answered by accounts that ex ante define the attributes of particular actors. Issues where there is no clearly defined knowledge community, issues where there are competing advocacy networks with rival claims to "moral" authority, issues where equally bureaucratic organizations vary in their authority: none of these issues can be readily analyzed through the tools of extant approaches. Equally important, none of these issues can be analyzed by simply discussing power and interests as though the content of their claims to authority were epiphenomenal. One cannot understand the course of disputes about population governance without paying close attention to the ways in which the discourse of demographers set the terms within which public health experts would have to make their case; nor can one understand the course of disputes about peacebuilding without paying close attention to the ways that a discourse centered on liberal values commands the heights of the field within which experts with immense local knowledge have to compete when trying to direct resources and shape policy. Content matters for Sending in a way that it simply does not in most other accounts, and this focus allows him to analyze and explain shifts in key policy areas without having to first identify a relatively stable consensus among experts that would only then begin to assert its effects in debates and discussions. Instead, contestation is ongoing, and explanation of any particular outcomes demands detailed consideration of the specific ways that the different types of knowledge and claims to authority in question have been and continue to be shaped by struggles for recognition among would-be experts.

In so doing, Sending has produced a remarkable book that makes an insightful, multifaceted contribution to our understanding of our contemporary global situation. In the end, that is what critical social science is *for*.

Patrick Thaddeus Jackson
Associate Dean for Undergraduate Education
School of International Service, American University

Acknowledgments

I gratefully acknowledge the financial support of the FP7 large-scale integrated research project "GR:EEN—Global Re-Ordering: Evolution through European Networks," European Commission Project 266809. I also received support from the Training for Peace project at the Norwegian Institute of International Affairs, and the Kjetil M. Stuland Research Prize has allowed me to travel to conduct interviews in Liberia, South Sudan, and New York. I would also like to thank my colleagues at the Norwegian Institute of International Affairs, where I have worked for almost all my career.

I have presented early drafts of different chapters at the following institutions, and I thank the organizers for inviting me and participants for their helpful comments: Oslo University College, UC Santa Cruz, UC Berkeley, McGill University, Brown University, Copenhagen Business School, University of Birmingham, and Institut Barcelona d'Estudis Internacionals.

I have received an extraordinary number of good comments and suggestions from colleagues at home and abroad on drafts of different parts of the manuscript. I thank Tanja E. Aalberts, Morten Skumsrud Andersen, Jacqueline Best, Morten Bøås, Andre Broome, Benjamin de Carvalho, Charlotte Epstein, Christoffer Conrad Eriksen, Niel Fligstein, Nina Græger, Stefano Guzzini, Kristin Marie Haugevik, John Karlsrud, Erlend Grøner Krogstad, Halvard Leira, Kristoffer Liden, Jon Harald Sande Lie, Mikael Rask Madsen, Frederic Merand, Anders Molander, Abraham Newman, Vincent Pouliot, Simon Reid-Henry, Pernille Rieker, Kristin Bergtora Sandvik, Niels Nagelshus Schia, Francesco Strazzari, Henrik Thune, and Eleni Tsingou. A special thanks to Iver B. Neumann, Leonard Seabrooke, and Stein Sundstøl Eriksen for our continued conversations about the questions addressed in this book.

Melody Herr, acquisitions editor at the University of Michigan Press, has been extraordinarily supportive and patient throughout the whole process, and I am greatly indebted to her. As series editor, Patrick Thaddeus Jackson has similarly been an enthusiastic supporter, offering extremely helpful comments along the way. Thanks also to the anonymous reviewers who read the whole manuscript and offered critical and important comments. Thanks are also due to Susan Cronin and Mary Hashman whose professionalism and expedience in getting the manuscript ready for print are greatly appreciated.

Research assistance from Wrenn J. Lindgren was very helpful, as was help from NUPI's language editor, Susan Høivik. Most of all, Joakim Hertzberg Ulstein has been invaluable in helping with language, sources, formatting, and insightful comments.

My friends have been very supportive, even interested, in this project. Thank you all! A special thanks to Bjarne Lie, who made the office space of Verdane Capital available to me when I needed time to focus on writing, and to Jon Fossen Thaugland, who sat me down at a critical juncture and said—in a way that only he can—enough is enough, finish the book.

And then, most important, my family: Your support and encouragement mean everything. And to Siri Jo—you have helped me in more ways than I can possibly acknowledge.

PART I

Introduction

Authority in Global Governance

Professionals mark global governance at every turn: they model and govern the economy; they make and interpret laws, fight wars, deliver humanitarian relief, and establish standards for everything from accounting to environmental conservation. An increasingly voluminous literature has emerged over the last two decades under the heading of *global governance* to describe and explain who these actors are, what they do, and how they shape contemporary world politics. We know, for example, that advocacy groups and expert groups can shape policy in important ways. We also know that associations of businesses can be important in developing industry standards which then become de facto global standards. And we know that international organizations are often decisive actors in their own right in formulating and implementing global rules. This literature has been important in part by demonstrating that a mix of both state and nonstate actors are involved in and have authority over questions of what is to be governed, how, and why.

But while theorists of global governance have excelled in their demonstration of the attributes and authority of these actors, they have largely done so by using analytical tools that fail to explain how these actors become authoritative. This omission stems from a particular framing of the study of global governance: analysts have honed their theoretical tools around particular *types* of actors. By using analytical tools that a priori privilege or single out one type of actor (experts, international organizations, advocacy groups, and so forth), one effectively reads out how authority is established through ongoing competition between a broader set of actors. Indeed, theories that are focused on actors' attributes assume away a large part of the puzzle that they want to address inasmuch as the analyst defines in advance those attributes that are assumed to be associated with a claim to authority, be it expertise, moral standing, capacity, or legal rationality. The epistemic communities approach (Haas 1992), for example, offers criteria by which to identify the existence of an epistemic community (shared knowledge base and policy objectives) but no tools with which to construct an analytically informed account of the relative importance of other actors, how a consensus emerged so that an epistemic community did form, and how this particular group prevailed over others to become recognized as an authority. Similarly, an analysis that is organized around the attributes of international organizations (IOs) and their sources of authority (Barnett and Finnemore 2004) is well suited to demonstrate that IOs often have considerable sway over states in how to define problems and suggest policy responses. But it is poorly equipped to assess why some IOs are authoritative while others remain marginal, as such an analysis necessitates a focus not on an IO's attributes per se but on its relationship with other actors and on how an IO's authority was initially constructed. Finally, advocacy groups are often said to be powerful actors in world politics by virtue of their moral authority (Risse 2012). But only those who share the moral values of such an advocacy group can be said to defer to their (moral) authority (Friedman 1990), and so it does not help us to account for why a particular group or actor became recognized to speak for and articulate those moral values that underwrites such a position of authority in the first place.

Competing for Authority

The goal of this book is to present and apply a framework for theorizing global governance as an ongoing process of competition for the authority to define what is to be governed, how, and why. I shift away from a focus on the attributes of predefined actors that engage in global governance and toward a focus on the dynamics by which authority is constructed and institutionalized and may be eroded. Such a focus allows me to account for how and why some actors rather than others become authoritative. It also opens up analyses of how the substantive contents of governance arrangements are products of the competition over positions of authority.

Two analytical moves are important here. First, I foreground the similarities rather than the differences between actors who represent or work for advocacy groups, expert groups, international organizations, and states. These actors are all engaged in efforts to fix and universalize the meaning of governance objects on behalf of and for others, and they draw on different resources and organizational loci for doing so. I therefore treat all types of actors engaged in efforts to shape the contents of governance as professionals—what Bigo (2011, 248) calls "transnational guilds of professionals"—whose identities and behavioral patterns cut across analytical categories of epistemic communities, international organizations, or advocacy networks (cf. Seabrooke 2014; Seabrooke and Tsingou 2009). I thus seek to avoid prejudging the positions and possible authority of any one type of actor, including state actors. As I demonstrate in chapters 4 and 5, for example, the field of population governance emerged and became institutionalized long before any state actors became heavily involved, and when states did become involved, state actors' positions were determined less by the fact that they represented a territorially delimited constituency than by their recognized competence and attendant resources among other professionals within an already institutionalized area of governance.[1]

Second, I develop a sociologically informed account of authority. Most accounts that invoke authority as an analytical category do so with reference to ideal-typical sources or forms of authority, be it expert authority, moral authority, delegated authority, institutional authority, or other (Avant, Finnemore, and Sell 2010). These distinct sources of authority are typically linked to and made an attribute of a particular type of actor (Barnett and Finnemore 2004; Risse 2012). But to say, for example, that an expert group has "expert authority" or that an advocacy group has "moral authority" is descriptive and classificatory, not explanatory: to the extent that authority is a relationship where one (subordinate) actor defers to another (superordinate) actor, we should be able to account for the mechanisms through which such deference is established and perpetuated and may be undone (Hopgood 2009). Moreover, a "source" of authority is not just there for an actor to draw on but must itself be constructed, nurtured, and made effective in particular settings. As I show in chapter 2, for example, an explanation of how the UN Secretariat emerged in a position of authority to design and manage peacekeeping operations cannot rest solely on a description of the Secretariat's bureaucratic attributes or other ideal-typical sources of authority (delegation, expertise, and so forth). Rather, we must account for how the Secretariat established itself with a recognized competence on and authority over things international through deliberate efforts to construct a new realm of governance—the international—that was distinct from member states' converging interests. The bureaucratic attributes of the Secretariat, therefore, do not explain its authority. Rather, it is the result of a successful claim to authority that was initially rooted in a claim to represent the international in an impartial and neutral way (Orford 2011).

Analytical Framework

I construct an analytical framework drawn somewhat selectively from the sociology of Pierre Bourdieu (1984, 2000). Three concepts make up the core of this framework, and I briefly sketch their contents here to give a sense of the key argument in the coming chapters. These are fields, capital, and recognition. A field is an analytical concept that aims to capture how a social space is structured into distinct positions and attendant material and symbolic resources. With its focus on actors' positions relative to others within a social space of "organized striving" or "self-organized contestation," the concept of field treats actors as strategic and interest-driven but in ways that are specific and heavily conditioned by the configuration and dynamics of each field (Bourdieu and Wacquant 1992). It is a methodologically justified concept aimed at capturing the competition and relationships between actors in a structured social space, the sociogenesis of which (Gorski 2013) is central for the account of what is at stake in the field, including what types of resources or capital are effective within it.

Capital describes the resources of different types to which any given actor has access and that are recognized as relevant in any particular field (Bourdieu 1986). The distribution and type of capital is only accessible through an analysis of the initial differentiation or establishment of a field, hence the importance of analyzing its genesis. The efficacy of any type of capital is field-specific, so while a preponderance of economic capital is a central resource, it is only effective to the extent that economic resources can be translated into capital that is valued and recognized by others in any particular field. By focusing on capital and its distribution and use within distinct fields, I seek to assume as little as possible about the ostensible identity and power of different types of actors. In so doing, the question of which types of actors are authoritative, or what type of "sources" of authority is prevalent, emerges from the empirical analysis rather than being imposed as the analytical framework for this analysis.

Recognition is the engine behind field dynamics. It is the drive for recognition that explains why different actors—endowed with different resources (capital) and holding different positions in a field—advance different claims in an effort to be recognized by others for their distinct profile, position, and identity. Most important for the task at hand, it is the dynamics of recognition (and misrecognition)—so central to Bourdieu's account of the what he calls the "production of belief" and the sociology of symbolic domination—that delivers the tools with which to empirically account for how and why some actors "defer" to others (Bourdieu 2000; Steinmetz 2008). In a nutshell, I argue that those in a subordinate position within a field are complicit in the perpetuation of the authority of those in a superordinate position by virtue of seeking recognition on terms set by the latter.

Why It Matters

What type of knowledge can we expect to produce through such an analytical strategy? How does it differ from extant accounts of global governance? I want to highlight three distinct contributions. The first is to advance a view of authority that differs in one key respect from the conventional view, rooted in methodological individualism, where the central question is why an actor should defer to another. Posing the question in this way makes a lot of sense, since it brings out a critical angle on relations of super- and subordination and allows us to assess the grounds (beliefs) on which one actor defers to another. But it comes at the price of downplaying the fact that individuals are socialized into a world that is always already hierarchically structured: by emphasizing the idea that actors seek recognition, the question of authority is in a sense turned upside down, for it is now no longer a question of why one should defer—as deference is built into the very fabric of a hierarchically structured social life. Rather, the question is on what grounds recognition is sought and accorded from others and in particular how some actors are able to impose the evaluative criteria in accordance with which others are compelled to seek recognition.

The second is to advance fields as an organizing concept for analyses of global governance—highlighting how professional actors compete within social spaces with distinct stakes over what is to be governed, how, and why. This analytical strategy is important as a tool not only to move beyond a focus on types of actors but also to explore how the substantive contents of global governance are a product of the competition for authority. That is, most of the literature on global governance sees the relationship between the identity of those who govern and that which they seek to govern as an external one, where the identity of governance objects (economy, health, peace, humanitarianism) is exogenous to the analytical framework for understanding the identity, behavior, and authority of governance subjects (epistemic communities, NGOs, advocacy networks, international organizations, or states). Even an explicitly relational account of authority structures in global governance (Avant, Finnemore, and Sell 2010) limits the relationship to that between "global governors" and the constituencies that these (claim to) represent. I show that how the authority to govern is established within distinct fields has direct bearing on the identity of governance objects: the definition and meaning of any given task—humanitarian relief, peacebuilding, population, development, health—is endogenous to the process by which actors seek and are recognized as authorities on how to act on and/or represent others (Abbott 2005). Such a focus on the relationship between the competition for positions of authority and the contents of governance arrangements is important for more than scholarly reasons: political debates are centered on the contents of governance practices, their effects, and their legitimacy. As analysts, we should contribute to such debates by accounting for and thus unmasking the workings of power in the production and perpetuation of the dominant standards against which political claims are assessed and either accepted or dismissed by other groups (Eriksen and Sending 2013).

The third is to advance a more sociologically informed account of the role of expertise in shaping global governance. Expertise is considered a central ingredient of global governance, and references to epistemic communities (Haas 1992) are a commonplace in the literature on global governance, having acquired status as ontologically given units. As I explain in chapter 1, however, there is no "independent" (causal) role of knowledge as advanced by an identifiable group of experts on policy outcomes. Rather, governance is inherently bound up with knowledge claims about that which is to be governed (Mitchell 2001; Wagner 1994). There is consequently always some body of knowledge (scientifically produced or not) involved in claims about how to define and act on governance objects. The question of whether and how expert groups may shape policy is therefore subordinate to the question of the type and contents of knowledge that prevail as authoritative in shaping debates about what should be governed, how, and why.

Structure of the Book

The book is organized in three parts. In part 1, I set out the main tenets of the analytical framework. I start with a discussion of existing literature on global governance and conceptualizations of authority to situate the contribution of the book as a whole. I then move on to discuss how and why the literature on epistemic communities, advocacy networks, and international organizations—so often referred to as ontological givens in discussions of global governance—provides us with only a limited account of how and why the authority to govern is produced and sustained over time. I discuss the concept of authority in some detail and—building on Friedman (1990)—adopt a minimal definition that foregrounds its relational character, anchored in recognition. The chapter explains how and why the concepts of fields, capital, and recognition offer a good handle on how authority is established and with what effects on governance objects and the social organization of fields. I specify my conceptualization of fields as organized around concepts of governance about which actors advance different conceptions, and I operationalize Bourdieu's concept of symbolic capital—which is crucial for understanding relations of deference and thus authority—in terms of the criteria of evaluation (Steinmetz 2006) that prevail in any given field.

In part 2, I focus on the emergence of *international* authority. In chapter 2, I account for the initial construction of the UN Secretariat's authority to govern beyond the UN Charter. I detail the continuity from the League of Nations, which inaugurated the category of the "international civil servant" whose loyalty was to be "exclusively international." And I account for how Hammarskjöld as secretary-general established a level of authority for the UN Secretariat by appropriating a concept of the international that was distinct from the sum total of member states' interest.

In chapter 3, I move on to show how the genesis of the authority of the UN Secretariat has come to structure, in profound ways, the field of peace operations. Because the authority of the Secretariat is anchored in a particular concept of the international, present-day peace operations are managed within a *nomos* where the meaning and significance of local context of peace operations is a product of and systematically made subordinate to the concept of the international. This distinction between the international and the local runs through and organizes the field in terms of competition between staff employed by the Secretariat and the types of governing practices that are seen as relevant and important.

In part 3, I focus on *transnational* authority. In chapter 4, I explore the emergence of the transnational field of population beginning in the 1940s, and its institutionalization throughout the 1960s. The analysis centers on how the authority to govern reproductive behavior was established, without formal international consent, by a group of nonstate actors, mainly in the US. I explain how the field became transnationalized and how its boundaries and internal configuration were significantly shaped by a theoretical formulation—the theory of demographic transition—advanced by US demographers. In chapter 5, I explore how the genesis of the field structured its internal topography and its boundaries to the adjacent fields of health and development. I detail how the ongoing competition for authority within the field pitted health professionals and advocacy groups organized around women's health and rights against proponents of population control through family planning programs who sought to win recognition for their distinct conceptions of fertility governance. Finally, I show that the emergence of a "reproductive health and rights" approach at the 1994 Cairo conference—hailed as a paradigm shift produced by a transnational advocacy network—is more accurately understood in terms of how already dominant actors reengineered the field's evaluative criterion in an effort to perpetuate their position.

In the conclusion, I revisit some of the larger debates to which the book seeks to contribute, key among them how to conceptualize global governance. I also expand on some of the insights from the empirical chapters and reflect on the character of the professional actors who manage global governance. These actors thrive on the construction and deployment of categories and attendant governing practices that are justified and attain their meaning as efforts to help others, typically those who "cannot speak for themselves." The relative autonomy of all such fields, then, is in part a product of a differentiation from those who are the *objects* of governing efforts. These professionals invariably claim to represent and speak on behalf of others, invoking variable configurations of knowledge claims, normative ideals, or lived experience. In this perspective, the construction of and competition over positions of authority among professional groups in global governance rest on a much more fundamental claim to authority over those who are the objects of governance efforts but who are not participants in global governance.

CHAPTER I

Competing for Authority

Recognition and Field Dynamics in Global Governance

Global governance is made up of more or less distinct and autonomous fields whose logic and boundaries can be uncovered by analyzing their genesis. Within these fields, actors compete with each other to be recognized as authorities on what is to be governed, how, and why. Actors are compelled to seek such recognition in terms of any given field's dominant evaluation criteria. The contents of any given evaluative criterion vary considerably between fields, as I detail in the chapters that follow. It is thus an empirical question which particular configuration of actors (state representative, expert group, advocacy network, international organization, or other) will come to occupy a position of authority in any given field.

Thus conceived, authority is about relations of deference, but such deference is not produced by legitimate belief (Hurd 1999, 387–88) or by a social contract (Lake 2010, 595–96) but—paradoxically—by the constant search for recognition within always hierarchically organized social spaces (Markell 2003, 22–23): some actors succeed in presenting their interests and attendant categories as natural and universal rather than arbitrary and particular, thereby establishing for themselves an idea of sovereign agency while transferring to others the burden of having to orient themselves through and seek recognition from categories not of their own choosing. I show in chapter 4, for example, how a small group of US-based demographers prevailed over a range of other actors, authoritatively defining the problem of population growth in such a way that health professionals were relegated to a marginal position. It was simply not possible for health professionals to be recognized for their distinctive definition of reproductive regulation within the parameters of this field's evaluative criterion, defined by demographers. Then, in chapter 5, I show how that same field was later transformed through a relative loss of autonomy, enabling health professionals to undo the authority of demographers and forcing demographers to reorient themselves in order to safeguard their position in the field.

My point of departure is that while authority has been central to debates about global governance, its conceptualization leaves much to be desired. There has been a tendency to use typologies of sources of authority, link these to actor attributes, and then conclude that a specific type of actor has authority. But such a conceptualization fails to account for the fact that authority is a *relationship* between a superordinate and a subordinate actor. We thus lack a theory-based framework for empirically exploring how authority is constructed, through what strategies, and with what effects on the contents of governance. To construct such a framework, I draw extensively on the work of Pierre Bourdieu (1984, 1991, 2000), highlighting the dynamics of recognition and misrecognition as central to the constitution of authority within distinct issue areas, or fields. Actors engaged in global governance, I hold, compete with each other to be recognized as authorities on what is to be governed, how, and why. They make use of the material and symbolic resources available to them, seeking to win recognition for their distinctive conceptions of governance. This view of the constitution of authority in global governance has three significant implications.

The first is that authority here becomes the *explanandum*, so we need to situate authority within a larger analytical framework that moves beyond ideal-typical classifications of sources of authority. It is worth recalling that Weber's ideal-typical sources of authority formed part of a larger conceptual apparatus. In Collins' words, ideal types of authority "do not make much sense in the absence of a larger network of concepts" (1986, 6). We need to place the exploration of authority within such a larger network of concepts and bring it to bear on global governance. The aim is to explain the competition between different actors over what counts as a "mark" of authority in particular contexts. If one given expert group is found to have authority in an issue area, we should ask why that particular group or constellation of actors and not some other constellation of actors came to win recognition as authoritative.

The second implication is that we cannot use analytical tools that are organized around and thus a priori privilege specific types of actors—be they states, international organizations, advocacy groups, or expert groups. We need a framework that shifts the focus from actors' attributes to their positions relative to others and the resources they bring to bear in the competition to be recognized as authoritative. International organizations (IOs) often have authority—but an analysis focused on IO attributes cannot explain why equally expert-driven and rule-following IOs have variable authority across different issue areas or why some state actors have almost complete control in some issue areas while remaining comparatively marginal in others.

The third implication is a theme that occupied Weber (1978) in his exploration of authority: how the source of an actor's authority gives rise to distinct forms of rule (Onuf and Klink 1989). With a few exceptions (Avant, Finnemore, and Sell 2010), extant literature has been content to demonstrate that particular types of actors have authority without exploring how an actor's source of authority is integral to and structures the type of rule and contestation associated with it. Put differently, the processes by which authority is constructed and the defining features of specific actors' authority are *endogenous* to the conceptions of governance advanced by that actor. When, for example, the UN Secretariat has authority over a given set of tasks—such as peacebuilding—we should locate the explanation of how the project of peacebuilding is defined and performed with reference to the genesis of the Secretariat's authority.

I proceed in three steps. First, I identify some limitations in accounts of global governance that can be attributed to their actor-centric analytical frameworks. Second, I discuss the concept of authority in some detail, arguing that it refers to recognized relations of deference between a superordinate and subordinate actor. Third, I present and justify a relational, sociological framework where authority emerges out of the ongoing competition for recognition within social spaces defined as fields. I hold that this framework can offer a better account of the establishment and effects of authority, that it can assess the relative importance of types of actors, that it links a concern with "who governs" directly to the substantive content of global governance arrangements, and finally that it allows us to compare the distinctiveness of issue areas (or fields) in global governance in terms of their genesis, social organization, and claims to authority.

Theorizing Global Governance

As early as in 1971, Joseph S. Nye and Robert O. Keohane noted the importance of exploring the power and role of nonstate actors in shaping foreign policy and the operations of international organizations (331). Two decades later, James Rosenau (1992) introduced the term "spheres of authority" as an analytical tool so as not to prejudge the dominance of states in the analysis of governance arrangements beyond the state. And more recently, the massive literature on global governance has produced a wealth of insights about the role, power, and effects of nonstate actors in world politics (Kahler and Lake 2003). In this literature, the concept of authority is crucial. While both David Lake (2009) and Stephen Hopgood (2009) are correct in noting that the assumption of anarchy in IR theory has meant that there has been a relative dearth of explorations of authority as an integral and systemic feature of world politics, students of global governance have put it to use to explore the role and importance of a myriad of different types of actors. Analysts have focused on the authority of international organizations (Barnett and Finnemore 2004; Weaver 2008), nongovernmental organizations (Bernstein and Cashore 2007), professional associations and expert groups (Cross 2013; Haas 1992), advocacy networks (Carpenter 2010; Keck and Sikkink 1998), and private corporations and their associations (Cutler 2002).

I identify some of the limitations of extant approaches, highlighting both what these should, by their own admission, be able to account for but cannot and what we should be able to account for that falls outside their remit. On the first score, we need to account for how and why one particular actor or configuration of actors emerges as authoritative. To include *authoritative* as part of the very definition of an actor will not serve to account for how that actor *became* authoritative. Nor does linking any type of actor to a particular source of authority constitute an explanation of the authority of any particular type of actor within a given issue area. On the second score, I extend the analysis of authority, exploring the Weberian question of how particular types or sources of authority give rise to distinct forms of governance or rule.

Actors and Ideal-Typical Sources of Authority

If there is one topic that is consistently brought to the fore in discussions of nonstate actors' sources of authority, it is that of *expertise*. Because of the general belief in the institution of science as setting rules for truth-seeking practices, scientifically produced knowledge is a central source of authority (Toulmin 1992; Wagner 2001; Wagner, Wittrock, and Whitley 1991). Reviewing the literature on transnational actors, Richard Price (2003, 587), for example, highlights expertise as a key source of authority. Similarly, in their edited volume on private authority in global governance, Rodney Bruce Hall and Thomas Biersteker (2002, 14) identify expertise as a hallmark of the authority of private, or nonstate, actors. By far the most influential account of the role of expertise in global governance is the *epistemic communities* approach expounded by Peter M. Haas (1992). Its standing as an account of the knowledge-policy nexus is such that "epistemic community" has taken on the status of an ontological given actor whose influence is assumed rather than demonstrated (Beyer 2007; Biersteker 1992; Drezner 2007; Rosenau 1999). In discussing international legal theory, for example, José E. Alvarez (2002, 150) refers to epistemic communities as having the same ontological status as international organizations.

The epistemic communities approach seeks to account for the role of experts in shaping "how states identify their interests and recognize the latitude of action deemed appropriate in specific issue-areas of policymaking" (Haas 1992, 2). Haas defines an epistemic community as a "network of professionals with recognized expertise and competence in a particular domain and an authoritative claim to policy-relevant knowledge within that domain or issue-area" (3). With this definition, Haas places the explanatory focus on the process whereby experts *already recognized as having authoritative and policy-relevant knowledge* can shape state interests. State decision makers are assumed to be uncertainty-reducers as well as pursuers of power and wealth—and epistemic communities serve to reduce uncertainty by defining the problems attendant on policy solutions. The three core analytical concepts—uncertainty, interpretation, and institutionalization—capture the diffusion and institutionalization of already recognized authoritative knowledge claims (Haas 1992, 3–4). However, none of these concepts can explain how such knowledge claims came to be regarded as consensual, authoritative, or policy-relevant in the first place. Haas claims that the epistemic communities approach focuses on the "process through which consensus is reached within a given domain of expertise" (23). But the explanatory logic of the epistemic communities approach kicks in only *after* actors have produced a consensual knowledge base that is recognized as authoritative and policy-relevant. No analytical tools are offered to explain how a consensus was formed and why some actors (and not others) became recognized as authoritative. For example, Adler's (1992) analysis of the US epistemic community of arms-control experts that came to shape US policy details the process whereby this group emerged. But this account of the *formation* of an epistemic community and its position of authority operates outside the analytical tools offered by the epistemic community approach itself. It fails to explain how and why arms controllers rather than those who advocated armament and counterforce strategies emerged in a position of authority to have the ear of policymakers. Adler notes how a "political selection process determined the epistemic community's success" and that "the policymaker . . . served as judge, jury and, if necessary, executioner over the professional output of strategic theories" (1992, 124). In other words, the authority of an epistemic community was here a result of rather than a driver of a "political selection process." In a more recent effort to reconstruct the epistemic communities framework, Davis Cross (2013) proposes an important extension of this framework by expanding the definition of epistemic communities beyond scientific experts to include analyses of interepistemic conflicts and to study the conditions under which the influence of epistemic communities is more or less likely to be influential. And yet the core elements of Cross's reconstruction retain the original formulation, where an epistemic community is defined as *already* recognized with authority. She argues, for example, that "when a group of professionals with *recognized expertise* is able to speak with one voice, that voice is often seen as *more legitimate* because it is based on a well-reasoned consensus among *those in the best position to know*" (147; emphasis added).[1] In this way, authority is invoked as a constitutive element of this type of actor's centrality, but no explanation is offered as to how and why such authority was established in the first place.

IOs have authority in world politics. They set agendas, define categories, implement policies, and enforce rules with considerable discretion (Kahler and Lake 2003; Koremenos and Snidal 2001). The account offered by Michael Barnett and Martha Finnemore (2004) is here central. They see IOs as authoritative by virtue of being bureaucratic. Invoking ideal-typical sources of authority—legal-rational, expertise, and moral authority—they move on to highlight attributes of IOs that fit with these sources of authority: IOs are rule-following (legal-rational authority), they embed expertise (expert authority), and they advance shared social and political objectives (moral authority) (ch. 1). On this basis, they show that the World Bank and the IMF (see also Seabrooke 2006; Weaver 2008), the UN refugee agency, and the UN Department of Peacekeeping Operations all have authority (and pathologies) *qua* bureaucratic organizations. This potent classification of types of authority demonstrates that IO authority may be independent of delegation from states. However, it cannot account for the emergence and evolution of such authority, since authority—as a relational phenomenon—cannot be determined by looking at the attributes of one actor. None of this tells us how and why, for example, the UN Department of Peacekeeping Operations is authoritative on peacekeeping, while its sister organization, the UN Department for Economic and Social Affairs, is (almost) nowhere to be seen in the global governance of economic matters.[2]

The literature on advocacy groups similarly relies on an actor-centric analytical framework, aiming to link or identify a particular type of actor, via its attributes, to a source of authority. In his review of the literature of transnational actors, Price concludes that moral authority is considered a "prime factor in the influence of transnational activists. . . . [D]ecision makers and/or citizens often believe that activists are not only (objectively) right in the sense of providing accurate information but also morally right in the purposes for which such knowledge is harnessed" (2003, 589).[3] And Sikkink (2002) argues that transnational networks and advocacy groups have "acquired 'moral authority' as a power resource that gives them influence beyond the limited material capabilities," linking this moral authority to the attributes or qualities of these networks in terms of their impartiality, reliability, representativeness, and accountability (312–35). A closely related source of authority is said to accrue from the claim to represent those who cannot speak for themselves. This claim to represent and speak on behalf of others goes hand in hand with the claim to advance a shared common good or something of moral worth. As Risse, Ropp, and Sikkink (1999) note, "Moral authority is directly related to the claim by transnational civil society that it somehow represents the 'public interest' or the 'common good' rather than private interests" (186). But the claim to represent or advance the "public interest" is common to all groups that are engaged in global governance, so we are none the wiser as to why some groups succeed with such claims and others do not.

These works cover a range of actors and various types of authority. They nonetheless proceed through the same *type* of analysis: a particular type of actor is defined through a set of attributes; these attributes are then linked to a generic source of authority; and, having established this link, the researcher proceeds to explore the pathways through which this type of actor succeeded or failed in shaping policy in some way. But why approach the question of authority in such terms? Why organize the analytical tools around specific actors? The answer is in part found in these works' primary explanatory objective, namely to show that there is a broad array of actors that are significant and important in world politics. My point is that this analytical set-up comes at a cost. We are well advised to reflect here on McAdam, Tarrow, and Tilly's (2001) observation that the use of fixed categories of types of actors represents an undue simplification, for "movements, identities, governments, revolutions, and similar collective nouns do not represent hard, fixed, sharply bounded objects, but *observers' abstractions from continuously negotiated interactions among persons and sets of persons*" (12; emphasis added). In scholarly work on global governance, there has to date been little reflection on what is lost by choosing analytical categories that focus on actors' attributes. Somers and Gibson remind us what is at stake here:

> While a social identity or categorical approach presumes internally stable concepts, such that under normal conditions entities within that category will act predictably, the [relational, transactional] approach embeds the actor within relationships and stories that shift over time and space and thus precludes categorical stability in action. . . . The classification of an actor *divorced* from analytical relationality is neither ontologically intelligible nor meaningful. (1994, 65, 69; quoted in Emirbayer 1997, 288)

Rather than contributing to the ever-expanding typologies of types of actors and a classification of possible sources of authority, I opt for an analytical strategy that seeks to capture relations between actors and their ongoing competition for authority. This means that what actors do and who they are is to be determined through analyzing the particular social space in which they are situated, how they are related to other actors, and what resources they have. But before spelling out the details of this approach to the analysis of global governance, building on some of Bourdieu's central concepts, it is necessary to examine the concept of authority in greater detail.

Authority as Recognized Relations of Super- and Subordination

Recent advances in the study of global governance have brought the concept of authority more to forefront through sustained analytical discussions. Lake (2009) advances a contractual view of authority to explain stable hierarchies. Hurd (1999) has shown how the institution of sovereignty makes up an international authority structure—it is honored (most of the time) in the absence of coercion and incentives. Using analytical tools from political sociology and drawing on participatory observation in Amnesty International, Hopgood (2006) brings out how different claims to authority (moral versus political) may coexist within an organization, causing tension and conflict over how to nurture and use this authority. Others have explored how globalization reconfigures the constitution of authority within states (Abrahamsen and Williams 2010; Sassen 2007). The most sustained discussion of authority in global governance is arguably that of Avant, Finnemore, and Sell (2010), who seek to account for *who* become established with authority and how. They advance, as I do here, an explicitly relational view of authority focused on the relationship between those engaged in governance and the constituencies on which they depend for material and political support. This helps to show how authority is constituted through particular relations. Nonetheless, Avant et al. also rely on ideal-typical sources of authority as the basis for their framework. To show that what constitutes a source of authority is highly variable and at stake in the competition between different actors, I opt for an analytical strategy that centers on the search for recognition.

Inspired by Friedman's (1990) work, I adopt a minimal definition of authority as comprising a *relationship* between a superordinate and a subordinate actor that is *recognized* and where the latter *defers* to the former. I discuss the three core elements of authority—relationship, recognition, and deference—in some detail. In so doing, my aim is to show that analyses of authority should not be confined to the identification of generic and ideal-typical sources in terms of belief systems that serve to legitimize authority. We need to differentiate analytically between the recognition of subordinate and superordinate actors, on the one hand, and the act of deference on the part of the subordinate actor, on the other. As Friedman (1990) notes,

> To bring out the precise character and role played by the element of "recognition" or "belief" that a person is entitled to rule (or to speak) within the authority relation, it is necessary to observe that the relationship must possess another feature in addition to the element of deference. . . . And this is that there must be some public way of identifying the person whose utterances are to be taken as authoritative. . . . [S]ome public way of identifying authority is a *logical* requirement of deferential obedience wherever it is to be found in society. (68)

The upshot of this is that recognition of positions of authority should be kept analytically separate from deference. Without a clear sense of the importance of *recognition* in establishing relations of super- and subordination, it is difficult to get a sense of the distinctiveness of authority, since an exclusive focus on the source of deference on the part of the subordinate actor removes the superordinate actor from the equation. That is, by accounting for an actor's authority with reference to an already existing and thus exogenously given "source" of authority—which explains deference—the superordinate actor is presented as being passive rather than active in the construction of his or her very source of authority. Deference can be habitual or more reflexive, and it does not, as Friedman has noted, necessarily imply the "surrender of private judgment" (64). A subordinate actor may very well reflect on and assess the contents of a superordinate actor's prescriptions and disagree with it yet defer to that actor. In short, authority relationships "can involve different sorts of submission" (62).

Recognition features prominently in the literature on authority in global governance. Lake (2009) presents his social-contract-based conception of authority by noting that it "does not exist without recognition" (8). Similarly, Zürn, Binder, and Ecker-Ehrhardt (2012) justify their analytical distinction between authority and legitimacy by noting that it "implies two layers of recognition" (83). And according to Avant, Finnemore, and Sell, "Authority is created by the recognition, even if only tacit or informal, of others" (2010, 9–10). But in these analyses, there is scarcely any exploration of recognition as a constitutive feature of authority. Given its centrality to the founding of authority, we need to be able to identify and account for how recognition is awarded or withheld and with what effects. Once we have established that authority designates a relation that rests on recognition, it becomes easier to explore the analytically distinct sources or dynamics of deference implied by authority. Drawing on Bourdieu, I argue that *mis*recognition is central to the establishment and perpetuation of authority, since it helps explain the social dynamic by which deference is produced and reproduced. Authority, in this view, extends well beyond the conscious "surrender" of private judgment and the choice to desist justification. It also includes cases where "the grip that established authority structures has over a person's mind may be so complete that it does not occur to him that that structure could be judged in the light of any standard external to it" (Friedman 1990, 73).

I contend that there is a *constant search for recognition*, where subordinate actors are *complicit* in the maintenance of their own position of subordination *without* this being necessarily based on a belief in legitimacy. While all actors strive for recognition, some actors will always have access to more resources (material and symbolic) with which to impose the categories and evaluative criteria to which others must refer in seeking recognition from others. To the extent that these categories are *misrecognized* as naturalized or universal categories, the socially produced and contingent character of social life is suppressed, and subordinate actors help perpetuate the conditions of their own subordination by seeking recognition from and deferring to superordinate actors.

In advancing such a conception of authority, I seek to drive home a point made by Peter Blau (1963)—that Weber, in relying on ideal types and privileging the beliefs that legitimate authority, did not sufficiently address the "structural conditions" and the attendant social logic that give rise to authority (307). To remedy this, we need a shift in analytical focus from ideal-typical sources of authority to the claims advanced by various actors in their efforts to be recognized by others as authoritative. For example, we may very well link a diplomat or a legal scholar or an international civil servant to ideal-typical sources of authority (representation of state, expertise, and bureaucratic rule-following)—but this cannot tell us whether and how such an actor has authority in specific social settings or how this authority was initially established. In Biersteker's (2012) formulation, we should direct our focus to the "practices of making and recognizing claims of authority" (260). This entails shifting the focus toward the material and symbolic resources that actors can draw on to put forward claims to authority and the structure of the particular social setting in which such claims are made and assessed by others (Bourdieu 1984, 41; 1990a, 138; 2000, 166). Of central importance here is that authority designates a relationship where there is necessarily a "distinction between statement and speaker such that the *latter* can endow the former with its appeal" (Friedman 1990, 69). This privileging of the position of the speaker is in keeping with Bourdieu's conception in his critique of Austin and also Habermas for failing to acknowledge that the authority of speech acts cannot be understood in the absence of an account of the social position of the speaker (Guzzini 2013, 83).

This is a crucial point, as any attempt to specify and account for authority necessitates a primary focus on how relations of super- and subordination are established and what gives the former the ability to induce deference in the latter. As Friedman (1990) notes, "The concept of authority can thus have an application only within the context of certain socially accepted criteria which serve to identify the person(s) whose utterances are to count as authoritative" (71). That is, we need analytical tools that can capture the "socially accepted criteria" that identify persons in authority—and such criteria cannot be Weberian ideal types of "sources" of authority, because these do not say anything about the criteria by which actors who put forth claims to authority are evaluated by others.

Fields and Authority

With its relational ontology and its focus on actors' positions relative to others within a social space of "organized striving" or "self-organized contestation," field theory depicts actors as strategic and interest-driven but in ways that are specific to each field (Bourdieu 1987, 1994; see also Martin 2003).

A field is a set of "relations between positions anchored in certain forms of power (or capital)" and a "network, or configuration, of objective relations between positions" (Bourdieu and Wacquant 1992, 16, 97). A field is a mesolevel order that mediates external events, transforming and filtering them according to field-specific features. It aims to capture social space as a social topography where actors occupy distinct positions based on the amount and type of resources (capital) that they have relative to others and as a space of contestation and competition over the meaning and stakes of the organization of this social space in terms of the symbolic categories through which it is defined. In other words, the synchronic view of the field as a space with distinct positions is coupled with a diachronic view of how it has evolved over time—the present configuration of any given field being seen as the outcome of past struggles (Gorski 2013, 329). By focusing on the dynamic competition between actors within an already structured social space, Bourdieu seeks to bring into view both the subjectivist (phenomenological) analyses of the categories used by actors to understand and act in the world and the objectivist (structural) analyses of the social conditions (positions) that facilitate the production of these categories (Bourdieu 1985, 727–28; cf. Pouliot 2007). This is central because it brings out Bourdieu's specific conception of the *social* (structured and competitive) construction of the categories through which social reality is presented as given (cf. Guzzini 2000).

Fields, then, make up relatively autonomous social spaces inasmuch as they are defined by and revolve around specific stakes and function according to specific laws that cannot be reduced to the field's environment. All fields are defined by actors' investment in what the field is about—what Bourdieu (1993) calls the *illusio*—the "objective complicity which underlies all the antagonisms" (73). In that sense, actors share an interest or belief in the importance of what the field is about, and this is expressed, as I see it here, in a shared concept of an object of governance, such as security or health, around which the field is organized. But among participants in a field, there are differing conceptions and attendant interests about how to define and govern that object of governance. As Bigo (2007) has noted, social spaces that have field properties have a "centripetal force" that attracts agents toward each other and which "is provided for by the specific stakes for which different agents act/play in order to win or resist" (239). At the same time, the shared interest and investment in the field is differentiated according to the specific positions and resources that participants can bring to bear. In Bourdieu and Wacquant's (1992) words, the shared interest in the game "differentiates itself according to the position occupied in the game" (117). Actors' interests and strategies are dependent on their position relative to others in the field, which is defined by their volume and types of capital: actors seek to "safeguard or improve their position and to impose the principle of hierarchization that is most favorable" to the capital that they possess (101). This implies first that the capital available to an actor is given by the structure of the field and second that field dynamics and changes in the field over time will hinge on how the "principle of hierarchization" is constituted and may be transformed. To get at the *logic* of a field, notably the specific purchase of different forms of capital, an objective mapping of the topology of a field and its positions must be matched by an analysis of the genesis of that particular field. That is, unless we know how the categories used to construct and divide the social world have come about, we have no way of knowing how some actors became authoritative in shaping the categories through which others also think and act in that world.

Recognition and Misrecognition

That the concept of fields denotes a social topography of different positions with attendant forms of capital (resources) linked to it is important as a first approximation of the competition for authority. But its purchase depends crucially on one additional element: that the competition within fields stems from actors' search for recognition. Bourdieu's stress on the dynamics of recognition and (mis)recognition is central to his sociological project. Not only does it underwrite his concept of symbolic capital, it is a fundamental tenet of his conception of social life in terms of the conceptual triad of field, capital, and habitus (Schiff 2014; Steinmetz 2008a). Here I adopt George Steinmetz's argument that the search for recognition is—and indeed must be—the engine of field dynamics and the role of different types of capital within it, although Bourdieu is arguably somewhat ambiguous on this score. In discussing recognition and misrecognition in Bourdieu's scholarship, Steinmetz (2006) concludes that Bourdieu has to presume a universalized drive for recognition in order to make his other concepts of field and capital work effectively to bring home the role of his most central concept—that of symbolic capital. In his words,

> Bourdieu instinctively falls back on a populist political vision that prevents him from noticing that his own concept of symbolic capital requires a universalization of the desire for recognition to all of the players in a social field. The dominated may develop a "taste for necessity," preferring their own (dominated) tastes to those of the elite.

But they recognize the dominant as holding more valuable cultural capital, that is, dominated and dominant recognize the same principle of domination. The dominant are granted recognition not just by their elite peers but also by the dominated participants in the field. (455)

Recognition dynamics holds the key for specifying the mechanisms through which relations of authority are established and perpetuated. What Steinmetz refers to as the "principle of domination" is the symbolic capital that prevails in any given field—what I, in the following, will call the field's criterion of evaluation to highlight that it serves as the standard against which hierarchies and thus authority are established and maintained. Because this evaluative criterion is shared by dominant and dominated alike— "the dominant are granted recognition not just by their elite peers but also by the dominated participants in the field"—we can see how relations of authority work in a way that typologies of types of authority cannot capture. Dominated or subordinate actors defer to the dominant not because of coercion or because of the incentives offered but because dominated actors deploy the resources at their disposal in an effort to be recognized by the evaluative criterion prevailing in the given field, and this evaluative criterion is, in fact, some actors' (particular) capital, misrecognized as the rules or standards against which all actors are evaluated.

Actors therefore care about, invest in, and compete over capital and its distribution because what is at stake is recognition from others. It makes sense to define fields as a "game" where all actors agree on the value of playing and where capital is what is deployed in the game only if the actors can be assumed to orient themselves toward others and seek recognition from them. An actor is "continuously led to take the point of view of others on himself, to adopt their point of view so as to discover and evaluate in advance how he will be seen and defined by them" (Bourdieu 2000, 166). It is, moreover, the drive for recognition that accounts for what Steinmetz calls the "doubling" of capital in Bourdieu's work: cultural capital, say, can be transformed into symbolic capital when and if it is recognized as authoritative and thus as defining the criteria for evaluating and distributing capital in a field. Holders of symbolic capital have power because they can impose their own categories as authoritative for the field as such: they have "obtained sufficient recognition to be in a position to impose recognition" (Bourdieu 1990c, 138). It is in this sense that symbolic capital implies recognition on the part of dominant actors and (mis) recognition on the part of dominated ones, as the latter help reproduce the criteria of evaluation that defines their subordinate position.

Understanding the dynamics of recognition helps us see that fields thrive on difference and differentiation rather than shared norms or a homogeneous discourse. With a shared interest in the stakes involved in the field, all actors search for recognition and seek to showcase their particular volume and species of capital. The drive for recognition therefore produces its own kind of integration within fields, since recognition is sought with reference to a shared concept of what the field is about, here defined as governance objects: A field is held together by a shared *concept* of what the field is about (security, health, development, etc.) but the different actors advance different *conceptions* of how to define and act on it. Precisely because actors seek recognition for their own positions, which are defined by the uneven distribution of capital, they differentiate themselves from others by showcasing their particular view on what is to be governed, how, and why. Actors are thus "necessarily involved in dynamics of recognition and competition, identification and dis-identification with other participants" (Steinmetz 2008a, 596).

This view of the struggle for recognition has its roots in Hegel's masterslave dialectic (cf. Buck-Morss 2009; Markell 2003). In Wendt's (2003) formulation, Hegel posited that "the effect of the struggle for recognition is precisely to transform egoistic identity into collective identity" (495; see also Greenhill 2008; Lindemann 2010). While space does not permit a discussion of the Hegelian logic of recognition or of Honneth's (1995) systematic reconstruction of the concept, it is important to stress that as conceived here, field-specific struggles for recognition do not produce collective identity in the form of internalized beliefs about what constitutes natural or appropriate courses of action. Wendt (2003) notes, for example, that "if the desire for recognition is about being accepted as different, the effect of mutual recognition is to constitute collective identity or solidarity" (512). This is because the Self is dependent on the Other for recognition: "Two actors cannot recognize each other as different without recognizing that, at some level, they are also the same" (512). As defined here, however, the effect of the search for recognition is not collective identity but actors' mutual interest and investment in what the field is about. By investing in efforts to gain recognition for their distinct conception of governance, competition between actors produces a level of integration, as the search for recognition implies a level of tacit, mutual recognition of others involved in the field. As Bourdieu (1998) notes about actors' investment in the stakes that define the field, "Interest is to 'be there,' to participate, to admit that the game is worth playing . . . it is to recognize the game to recognize its stakes" (77).

Authority and (Mis) Recognition

The constituting elements of authority are closely linked to the ways in which some actors are able to produce the very categories through which others see and understand the world—to what Bourdieu calls the "production of belief." Bourdieu builds on Cassirer's philosophy of symbolic forms and attempts to render it amenable to sociological analysis. Cassirer proposed that the sensed and experienced changes once it is related to concepts.[4] Bourdieu (1984) adds a clear sociological dimension to this view when he extends Durkheim's argument that symbolic forms are social forms by arguing that

> all knowledge of the social world, is an act of construction—implementing schemes of thought and expression. . . . [B]etween conditions of existence and practices or representations there intervenes the structuring activity of the agents, who, far from reacting mechanically to mechanical stimulations, respond to the invitations or threats of a world whose meaning they have helped produce. (466–67)

The centrality of analyzing the "production of belief" has to do with the ability of some actors to present and win acceptance for *their* categories (or social criteria)—necessarily structured by their own particular interests—as natural or universal ones: other actors misrecognize these categories as universal and naturalized, thereby conferring symbolic capital on some actors to produce the categories through which others understand and act in the world. For Bourdieu (1986), authority is therefore to be understood as a type of domination effectuated by the "production of belief" in which some forms of capital are "unrecognized as capital and recognized as legitimate competence, as authority exerting an effect of (mis)recognition" (49). The implication of this is that authority may exist without explicit legitimation (cf. Bugge 2007, 160; Zürn et al. 2012; Neumann and Sending 2010). More specifically, authority now emerges as a distinct relationship where, in Steinmetz's (2006) formulation, "dominated and dominant recognize the same principle of domination. The dominant are granted recognition not just by their elite peers but also by the dominated participants in the field" (455). For Bourdieu, this is intimately linked to the "political economy of symbolic violence" (Wacquant 2005a, 134)—where, as noted, some actors can present their particular interests as universal ones. But as Jade Schiff (2014, 130–31) argues, the concept of misrecognition should be broadened to include more than such an "ideological" component. It also includes—importantly—

what is forgotten and suppressed about the contingent and produced character of social life. It concerns the "amnesia of genesis" (Bourdieu 2004, 37) of those categories through which actors understand the world and act in it, which is the basis, for example, of the practice of gift exchanges (Bourdieu 1977, 171). That is, the sheer complexity of modern society puts a premium on categories that enables navigation and the reduction of uncertainty; such categories, which necessarily include some elements of social reality but not others, are the stuff of how actors get by and without being overburdened with reflexivity and complexity (Markell 2003, 22–23). This helps explain the nature and perpetuation of relations of authority inasmuch as the search for recognition within always hierarchically organized social spaces generate a dynamic where subordinate actors are complicit in the maintenance of their own position without this being based on a belief in legitimacy.

By investing in a field and subjecting to its forces, actors are compelled to seek recognition in terms prevailing in a field. Therefore, the element of deference that is implied by authority may be best understood in terms of the structuration of available conceptualizations with which to seek recognition. As we will see in chapter 3, for example, developing countries, and particularly those subject to peacebuilding efforts, are subjected to a category of the international through which they are monitored, assisted, and governed, and they must engage with this category to be heard or recognized. And in chapter 5, we will see how health experts in the field of population had to reckon with and seek recognition with reference to the already established categories and evaluative criterion that had come to define the field of population governance.

Fields and the Competition for Authority in Global Governance

I see three reasons why this perspective can yield new insights. First, analyzing the formation of a field—including how its boundaries, logic, and hierarchy were established—can yield important insights into how and why some groups have emerged with a dominant position relative to others. Second, by situating different actors within a structured social space, the relative role (and authority of) various constellations of actors (expert groups, advocacy groups, diplomats, international civil servants, and others), can be assessed by identifying what type of material and symbolic resources (capital) is efficacious, depending on the evaluative criterion of each field, rather than on predefined actor categories. Third, fields are mesolevel orders, so changes in a field over time are not attributed to overarching structures with their own logic or to the outcome of the interaction of independently constituted actors. Instead, changes are accounted for by focusing on the competition between different actors within the field—each with access to a differentiated set of resources—and to events external to the field that are always filtered and mediated by the field's distinct boundaries and setup. Thus defined, fields provide us with an analytical apparatus for analyzing the politics within and between relatively autonomous transnational governance fields such as "health," "development," "security," and "population" (cf. Fligstein 2002; Volberda and Lewin 2003).

Most fundamentally, by making a minimal assumption about the search for recognition, we get an empirical handle on the vexing question of how and why some actors, and not others, emerge in positions of authority. Authority is, as Hurd (2005, 502) has noted, always "under construction" because "communities are never unanimous in their assessment of the legitimacy of institutions." (502). But while there is no unanimity, some actors do have more resources (capital) than others to impose standards against which assessments of authority are made. Treating social spaces as fields organized in hierarchies makes it possible to analyze empirically who is in a position to grant and to withhold recognition. To explain why actor x is dominant and actor y is dominated within a given field, we must first analyze the genesis of a field and identify the field's symbolic capital—specified as the field's evaluative criterion—and then map how different actors have access to different types of capital and their attendant strategies for seeking recognition in keeping with the field's evaluative criterion.

As conceived here, fields are organized around governance objects. This means that their logic, boundaries, and social organization are closely tied up with how the objects of governance are defined. This is why attention to the epistemic authority is crucial. The contents of a body of knowledge—whether scientifically produced or not—that at some point t_0 become authoritative in defining what to govern, how, and why, will at a later point t_1 be reflected in the relations between actors, the boundaries to other fields, and the key points of contention within a field. This is not because the contents of authoritative claims about governance objects have at t_1 been internalized by all actors, as postulated by conventional constructivist theories, or have formed a discursive formation that sets up subject -positions defining what can and cannot be said and thought, as argued in post-poststructural accounts. Rather, dominant actors—armed with knowledge claims (cultural capital) (mis-) recognized as symbolic capital—can shape the field in two distinct ways: one generic to all fields, and one specific to fields as organized around governance objects. First, dominant actors can impose the criteria of evaluation that dominated actors must refer to and seek recognition in relation to. Second—and this is a feature of particular importance to fields of governance as conceived here—authoritative knowledge claims function not only as (mis-) recognized natural categorizations of the world, but as tools for purposively acting on it. Because a set of categories recognized as authoritative will be used to design and establish governing practices, social density and materiality are accorded to the dominant conception of governance by anchoring it in concrete governing practices and the attendant organizations with staff and technical artifacts that reflect, and thereby help naturalize, the categories that helped establish them. Bourdieu's (1994) formulation can stand as programmatic for the analysis that follows as it brings out the importance of unearthing the genesis of distinct fields:

> By realizing itself in social structures and in the mental structures adapted to them, the instituted institution makes us forget that it issues out of a long series of acts of *institution* (in the active sense) and hence has all the appearances of the *natural.* This is why there is no more potent tool for rupture than the reconstruction of genesis: by bringing back into view the conflicts and confrontations of the early beginnings and therefore discarded possibilities, it retrieves the possibility that things could have been (and still could be) otherwise. (1994, 3–4)

Because fields are organized around the construction and management of governance objects and driven by recognition dynamics, the approach offered here is less focused on ethnographically informed analyses of habitus. Like Pouliot (2008), I stress that what actors think about (governance objects) is shaped by where they think from (positions in a field), but with the difference that what they think from manifests itself through articulate, and more or less strategic, attempts at gaining recognition in the field, rather than in an inarticulate "practical sense." The approach formulated here thus shifts the accent slightly from socially produced drivers of action (norm internalization, habitus, discourse), to socially produced "tools" that actors use to gain recognition within fields (Swidler 1986; cf. Vaisey 2009).

PART II

CHAPTER 2

Diplomats, Lawyers, and the Emergence of International Rule

In this and the next chapter, I analyze the genesis and dynamics of a field of "international rule" that received its first expression with the League of Nations. The stakes in this field did not include claims to authority over any specific governance object such as fertility or health or development but rather the "international" as a social space distinct from the sum total of states' interests. The competition (of sorts) between lawyers and diplomats from the late nineteenth century onward introduced legally inspired categories of rule-based regulation, arbitration, and mediation to be used by diplomats (Kissinger 1994, 222). The establishment of the League and later the United Nations with "international civil servants" whose loyalty was to be exclusively to things international, is conceivable only with reference to the establishment of such a category of the international as a space to be regulated through rules. From the 1950s on, this formed the basis for the development of the UN Secretariat, with a significant yet circumscribed authority over the international.

In analyzing the formation of a field of international rule in this way, I am not suggesting that it was autonomous or that a distinct type of symbolic capital prevailed. If anything, the field in question was, and is, heterodox—characterized by a weak orthodoxy in terms of what the field is about (Gorski 2013, 130–31). Rather, I aim to show that there was an initial differentiation where some actors could claim competence on, and a certain level of authority over, the design and implementation of certain tasks in the name of the "international." While the claim to authority of international civil servants was initially over fairly specific and circumscribed tasks, it paved the way for a considerable expansion along similar lines in the following decades, to be explored in more detail in chapter 3. The analysis is geared toward demonstrating two main things: First, I seek to show that while we may treat international organizations (IO) as having rational-legal and expert authority (Barnett and Finnemore 2004), such categorizations do not explain how such authority was initially constructed or how the scope of such authority is linked to the conception of the social space of the international over which it is recognized as a bureaucracy. To explain an IO's authority, it is necessary not only to trace the particular genesis of the object of governance over which it became recognized as having authority but also to demonstrate which actors, drawing on what resources, prevailed to define or accord a particular international organization as being in a position of authority. Second, I seek to show what we gain by not taking established analytical categories of the international as our point of departure. Rather than imposing an analytical category of the international as, say, anarchic—from which it makes sense to ask why states cooperate and decide to set up international organizations (Keohane 1984; Rathbun 2012) or how states design them to further certain ends (Potter 1931; Schwebel 1994)—I seek to identify one specific interpretation of the "international" advanced by those engaged in debates about what could be governed in the realm between states. I show how the concept of the international that emerged from field-specific competition between diplomats, lawyers, and others prevailed to shape both the League of Nations and the United Nations.[1]

From the National to the International: Professional Authority beyond the State

The stakes in the formation of a category of the international on the basis of which a field of *international* rule would later emerge are distinct from the *transnational* field to be analyzed in chapters 4 and 5: a *transnational* field of population emerged from competing substantive claims about the causes and consequences of population change from the disciplines of economics, eugenics, demography, and health but within a shared framework of already presumed universal validity owing to the general belief in the institution of science to transcend national borders. Not so with the emergence of a field of international rule, in which the key professional groups involved, lawyers and diplomats, occupied positions of authority owing precisely to their respective national frames of reference, with no presumption that competing claims could or should be assessed within a shared and in principle universally valid epistemological framework. Granted, all professional groups owe their positions to their distinct national configurations (Fourcade 2009), but law is particular in that it is integral to the very process of state formation. Bourdieu, Wacquant, and Farage (1994) note, for example, that "juridical writings . . . take their full meaning not only as theoretical contributions to the knowledge of the state but also as political strategies aimed at imposing a particular vision of the state" (3). The authority of lawyers and of legal science, was initially tied to a national frame of reference: a recognized legal expert in the nineteenth century was an expert on national law, with little purchase on other countries' legal code (Koskenniemi 2001, 11–18). Similarly, diplomats operate in a framework of shared rules about how to negotiate with recognized others (Adler-Nissen 2014; Neumann 2013; Sharp and Wiseman 2007). The institution of diplomacy is based on the recognition of the particularity of the polities that make up the system: diplomats share a "thin" culture of protocol, mutual recognition of independence, and ways to communicate with recognized others (Sending 2011). In many ways, diplomats are to the outside of the state what lawyers are to its inside: recognized representatives of the state in dealing with concrete instances of conflicting interests, the management of which are recognized to demand certain skills. Because of this, the trajectory of the field of international rule—populated and institutionalized first and foremost by international organizations—is distinct in that it turned on the construction of the international as an object of governance, where an emerging cadre of international lawyers sought recognition from diplomats for their contributions to and relevance for managing interstate relations.

The word *international*, it bears stressing, entered English language much later than one would think. An early reference—reflecting on political rule—is found in Jeremy Bentham's (1789/1988, 326–27) *The Principles of Morals and Legislation*. It is no coincidence that it is introduced precisely in a discussion of the distinction between laws within and between states:

> The word *international*, it must be acknowledged, is a new one; though, it is hoped, sufficiently analogous and intelligible. It is calculated to express, in a more significant way, the branch of law which goes commonly under the name of the law of nations; an appellation so uncharacteristic, that, were it not for the force of custom, it would seem rather to refer to internal jurisprudence. The chancellor D'Aguesseau has already made, I find, a similar remark: he says that what is commonly called *droit* des *gens*, ought rather to be termed *droit* entre *les gens*. (327)

The concept of an international system—of a realm in which *relations between* sovereign states assume an independent and distinct existence—does not occur with the Treaty of Westphalia and the subsequent dismantling of the Roman Empire (Bartelson 1995, 139). Bartelson refers among other things to Pufendorf's (1660) *Elementorum Jurisprudentia Universalis Libri Duo*, in which Pufendorf remarks, "We are of the opinion that there is no law of nations, at least none which can properly be designated by such a name" (165 cited in Bartelson 1995). Bartelson's main contention is thus that "if we by international system mean a totality which is something *more than the sum of its constituent parts*, yet something presumably *distinct from* a universal *Republica Christiana*, we have to wait another 200 years for its emergence within political knowledge" (1995, 137; emphasis added). In exploring the emergence of a modern concept of the international, we have to look to the developments from the mid-nineteenth century onward. While the concept of the international as a space to be filled with rules owes its genesis to a range of factors, such as changes in the role of democratic publics in commenting on foreign policy, including the role of the press (Leira 2011), I here focus on how the concept of the international that prevailed at the Paris Peace Conference can be traced to the engagement between lawyers and diplomats over the character of the relations between states and what types of skills and competence were needed to regulate or act on these relations.

The Making of International Law and the Partial Transformation of Diplomacy

In mid-nineteenth century, international law was, in Koskenniemi's (2001) phrase, an "amateur science" (28): it was initially the province of philosophy and migrated to law faculties much later. When it migrated, international law was explicitly linked to humanitarian concerns, to diplomacy, and to the cause of peace: "If in France international law existed as a somewhat exotic branch of natural law and in Germany as an outgrowth of public law and diplomacy, in England there was virtually no university teaching in the subject in the first half of the century" (33). When such professorships were established in England from the late 1850s onward, they were not exclusively in international law but rather in international law in relationship to diplomacy and war. The chair at the University of Oxford was in international law and diplomacy, and the one at Cambridge was mandated to work for the extinction of war (Abrams 1957, 361). On a more general basis, lawyers were not initially recognized as having competence on interstate affairs.

In order to use their juridical capital to gain influence over the (relatively) closed realm over which diplomats claimed a recognized competence and authority, they sought to redefine this realm away from conceptions of absolute sovereignty and a strict inside/outside dualism. This was the context in which lawyers sought to bring legal concepts to bear on the realm between states and gain recognition for such skills among diplomats and elected officials. They did so by (a) drawing on the advocacy of peace societies while at the same time differentiating themselves from their "unscientific" arguments, (b) establishing learned societies to build a cadre of competent lawyers in different countries, and (c) circulating—drawing on their already established elite positions—among positions as law professors, diplomats, and politicians (cf. Madsen 2011).

The effort to establish a proper science of international law was inspired by broader developments in which public opinion grew more openly critical of the closed circuits of diplomacy (MacMillan 2007, 84–86). In the attempt to convert and adapt their specific sets of skills so as to make them an integral part of diplomatic practice, legal actors sought not so much to challenge and replace the position of the diplomat as to bring their skills and expertise to bear on interstate affairs. MacMillan (2007) notes how a growing middle class supported peace societies that preached the "virtue of compulsory arbitration of disputes, international courts, disarmament, perhaps even pledges to abstain from violence as ways to prevent wars" (85). In Britain, the elitism and secrecy of diplomats was often questioned and subjected to criticism in Parliament (Steiner 1969, 16–23). The impact on diplomats' position was significant in that key aspects of diplomatic practice "were increasingly questioned in domestic political circles" (Mösslang and Riotte 2008, 12), and while their general position was not threatened, the content of their practice—the skills deemed necessary to engage other countries to represent interests and avoid war—surely was.

In this context, a series of initiatives were made across the Atlantic to bring international lawyers together with those organizing peace societies. Peace societies wanted to "legislate [peace] into existence" (Abrams 1957, 380). Inspired by religious beliefs, they saw the rule of law more as God's will, while law societies were more prone to establish peace through the science of law, engaging in codification and in arbitration. As MacMillan (2007) notes, in the US, the League to Enforce the Peace had bipartisan support, while in Britain, a League of Nations Society "drew a respectable middle-class, liberal membership" (87). In France as well, government-appointed commissions were established to analyze how best to organize international society after the war, with the French proposal including suggestions of a standing army and the British proposal including suggestions of mandatory arbitration of disputes (87).

James B. Miles, secretary of the American Peace Society, traveled to Europe to enlist the support of international lawyers there for a congress to be held in the US under its auspices. The successful arbitration of the *Alabama* case between the US and the UK was seen as an ideal platform for the next step in such a development—to codify legal rules to regulate interstate affairs and so move beyond the peaceful settlements of disputes through arbitration. In this endeavor, the organizers believed that a "Senate of Jurists" could formulate an international legal code, and the "reputation of the distinguished authors of the code would be enough to ensure its acceptance by the governments" (Abrams 1957, 364). Gustave Rolin-Jaequemyns and Gustave Moynier declined the invitation to join the conference of the American Peace Society, opting instead to establish the Institut de Droit International (IDI) in 1873. This was a project aimed at the "study and promotion of international law" rather than advocacy for international law to replace politics (370). In the *Revue de Droit International*, the journal of IDI, Rolin-Jaequemyns wrote that the IDI was to engage in "collective scientific action" in an effort to work for the establishment of an international "society of law" (371).

The decision to differentiate their legal cum political project from the work of peace societies was seen by the key figures in the American Peace Society as a rebuff. For international lawyers like Rolin-Jaequemyns, however, peace societies had "never sufficiently distinguished law from ethics, sentimental aspirations from exigencies of practical reason" (quoted in Abrams 1957, 363). The establishment of IDI was based on a dual strategy: first, to establish a position from which to speak authoritatively on international politics, and second, to do this by following a professions-based trajectory—establishing a cadre of international lawyers who would be recognized as competent to interpret, develop, and apply legal rules to avoid war. The IDI had some success in this regard: it was awarded the Nobel Peace prize in 1904, drafted the language for the legal framework of the protection of the Suez Canal, and devised the procedures for arbitration that were used at the Hague Conferences (Abrams 1957, 380; Koskenniemi 2002, ch. 1). As such, the IDI would prove critical, for it would develop to form the most prestigious place for discussions of international law, one that was organized around the goal of codification as a stepping-stone to fill the international realm with rules to regulate the relations between states. As Sacriste and Vauchez (2007) have shown, the IDI was instrumental in establishing international lawyers as the prime contenders to diplomats' position as authorities on international affairs. It served both to validate legal competence and to build an international network of lawyers committed to international rule of law (88). As they note, "IDI could collectively guarantee that its members could rely on both technical skills and a reputation of independence from political and diplomatic games," so the organization was recognized as the "natural breeding ground capable of providing, on a larger scale, the umpires needed to manage international politics' conflicts" (99).

It is important to stress that such a claim to authority on the part of international lawyers to manage interstate relations did not solely emanate from some idea about the authority of law in general. Rather, through the circulation between positions in academia, on courts, and in diplomatic circles, lawyers could "collectively claim many *political* credentials" (Sacriste and Vauchez 2007, 98). The authority of international law is thus here linked to the position of authority of international *lawyers* as participants in diplomatic practice, where they seek recognition for their skills and tools as relevant for diplomacy. Sacriste and Vauchez link this role of lawyers to the establishment of a distinct "peace technique," the essence of which was codification and application of rules as a tool to manage interstate relations. And this technique was, in turn, premised on their claim to neutrality and independence:

> In an international scene still dominated by the confrontation of national interests, the scarcity of this "independent" profile was the best warrant of the value of such legal expertise. This specific authority these international lawyers successfully claimed . . . was the outcome of two elements: first, the social capital this emerging legal community managed to put together under the flag of the cause of IL and, second, the then growing demand in international politics for mediation and conciliation. (97)

This "peace technique" gained prominence through the establishment of the Permanent Court of Arbitration in 1899, the Hague Peace Conferences in 1899 and 1907, and the Geneva Conventions of 1864 and 1906 (Best 1999). The president of the 1899 Hague Conference, His Excellency Staal, noted that "diplomacy is no longer merely an art in which personal ability plays an exclusive part; its tendency is to become a science which shall have fixed rules for settling disputes" (quoted in Reus-Smit 1999, 122). This reflected international lawyers' relative success in being recognized as competent to analyze and regulate interstate relations. Between 1892 and 1920, for example, every US secretary of state with the exception of one was a prominent member of the American Society for International Law (Wertheim 2012). And in Paris in 1919, the commission tasked with producing a draft of the Covenant of the League, chaired by US president Wilson, was made up of prime ministers and foreign ministers from the US, Britain, Italy, Belgium, Brazil, China, Serbia, and Portugal, almost all of whom had a law degree.

The setup of the Versailles Conference reduced the purchase of distinct legal capital relative to that of diplomats and political leaders (despite their law degrees): these negotiations were undertaken not by actors qua lawyers but by diplomats with legal competence. Likewise, it was clearly distinct from the dynamic of study groups and background studies conducted by IDI, the American Society for International Law, and the International Law Association. Legal categories pervaded the negotiations, but legal capital as such did not affect the relative positions of each actor in the negotiations. In Stephen Wertheim's (2012) interpretation,

> British representatives and US President Woodrow Wilson privileged politicians' judgment above judicial settlement. Lawyers had to get out of the way of politicians attuned to popular sentiment, the true agent of historical progress. The League's central institution became parliaments of politicians, embodied in the Executive Council and Assembly. The well-known rejection of the Hague legacy at Paris therefore had less known material consequences: it spurned not only prior ideas but also contemporaneous proposals to extend Hague efforts radically and to take international society in a more formal and juridical direction. (213)

This interpretation nonetheless downplays how the design of the League of Nations was based on thinking about the space between states as one to be filled with legal rules, a task that necessitated a cadre of actors capable of implementing and managing rules in an impartial and neutral way.

Legal Categories and the Raw Material of International Authority: International Civil Servants

Sir Eric Drummond, the secretary-general of the League of Nations, is credited with designing the League with a permanent secretariat modeled on the British civil service. This was not a foregone conclusion, however. At least two models were on the table. There was what we today call a "transgovernmental" model, drawn from the experience of wartime cooperation, in which national representatives were to meet their counterparts from other states on a regular basis to coordinate with each other and to agree on future courses of action. This model was in part also based on technical cooperation that had already been developed through such organizations as the Universal Postal Union, founded in 1874, and the Office International d'Hygiène Publique, founded in 1907. It pointed in the direction of developing a loosely coordinated system of technically delimited cooperation. The Fabian Society in the UK, for example, observed that there was an emerging pattern of international government already being established for the purpose of technical cooperation and argued that an international authority to prevent war should be "based upon an amalgam of national and functional institutions" (Dubin 1983, 470). This model implied a system of international rule where the distinction between national and international is circumvented through direct contact and collaboration, across borders, between actors within similar professional categories (i.e., economists, health professionals, lawyers), whose very professions carry the potential for international rule (cf. Fourcade 2006). A particular version of this model was advanced by Sir James Arthur Salter, an economist. Seeking explicitly to secure a prominent position for economists and the Treasury relative to the Foreign Office in coordinating government policy, he argued for a system of national representatives to coordinate closely with each other and the Secretariat in Geneva. In his view, "The Foreign Office representing a specific point of view as the Treasury does, but not being the sole medium of communication" (quoted in Dubin 1983, 475). Salter's conception thus included the proposal that the League had to be run not only by the "non-national staff of the Secretary-General" but by "national secretariats composed of persons enjoying the confidence of their own governments and fully knowledgeable about national policies" (475).

This conception of international rule is based on a distinct view of the competencies and skills deemed necessary to govern. International rule is here seen to be best served by bringing together professionals within distinct issue areas—to transnationalize already shared substantive expertise and competence such as that possessed by established professions. E. J. Phelan, writing from his position at the International Labour Organization (ILO), captured an important element of this model when he claimed that "the technician has in certain fields replaced the diplomat" (1933, 310).

The secretariat model that prevailed, by contrast, was drawn mainly from the British idea of a civil service with a permanent staff, organized hierarchically, to offer support in the daily work of the organization and to implement decisions. Rather than international rule being anchored in a preexisting transnational network of functionally defined experts, as in the ILO model, or in national representatives or liaisons meeting permanently in Geneva with the support of a small conference secretariat, the very category of the international came to define, however loosely, the social space in which the Secretariat was to operate. And this category of the international followed from the prolonged engagement between diplomats and lawyers, where the latter did succeed in gaining a level of recognition for conducting diplomacy through the application of rules.

The social space in which such rules were to be applied rested on a conceptual aggregation from the national to the international: international law was seen as "a spontaneous outgrowth of society" and as reflecting a "cosmopolitan order," and the international lawyer was assumed to be "an organ of popular conscience-consciousness" (Koskenniemi 2002, 54, 53). Despite important differences in distinctively national traditions of conceptualizing international law, these international lawyers "took it upon themselves to explain international affairs in the *image of the domestic State, governed by the Rule of Law.* For that purpose, they interpreted diplomatic treaties as legislation, developed with a wide and elastic doctrine of customary law, and described the state as an order of competences, allocated to the state by a legal order" (361; emphasis added).

It was this category of the international that defined the conditions of possibility for the design of the League Secretariat around the principle of impartiality and of international loyalty. As Openheim (1919) noted in his lectures following the establishment of the League, "Any kind of an International Law and some kind or other of a League of Nations are interdependent and correlative" (6, quoted in Kennedy 1986, 903–4). The discussions in 1919 took place on the terrain of a set of categories that defined the international as a realm that could and should be filled with legal rules, the disagreement being over whether this should proceed through legal reasoning or diplomatic practice. As Lord Cecil's secretary summarized the discussions over the design of the League, "The real divergence lay between the adherents of the rigid, the definitive, the logical, in other words, the juridical point of view, and those who preferred the flexible, the indefinite, the experimental, the diplomatic" (920). The latter position prevailed, yet the composition and working methods of the League Secretariat are best described as bringing together both types of competence and skills: the key features of the Secretariat were that it was to be an *international* bureaucracy, with diplomatic skills seen as key to the task of advancing rules to regulate interstate affairs.

A key aspect of the secretariat model was that the League was to have a permanent staff whose members would divest their national loyalty and have an exclusively "international" loyalty. The relationship between the national and the international emerges as that which set the Secretariat apart from its member states; the differentiation of the international would here be made manifest in the establishment of a distinct entity. As suggested by Drummond and approved by the Balfour Report on the design of the Secretariat, "Members of the Secretariat once appointed are no longer the servants of the country of which they are citizens, but become for the time being the servants only of the League of Nations. . . . The members of the staff carry out . . . [n]ot national but international duties" (quoted in Schwebel 1994, 248). The resulting Secretariat mirrored a national civil service in that it was organized into sections that each covered functional areas (Drummond 1931, 228). There was no specification of the type of professional competence required for its staff, only that they were to be competent and to have an exclusively international orientation. The so-called Committee of Thirteen, set up to specify the regulations for the Secretariat, argued that the Secretariat should have a stable cadre of international civil servants and should draw on specialized expertise where necessary so as to balance the stable element of the ideal "international man . . . committed to the strictest and most scrupulous impartiality in examining and solving all problems submitted to it; while the other would be temporary and specialized, freer in judgment and able to modify solutions as to make them acceptable to the various nations" (quoted in Ranshofen-Wertheimer 1945, 29). The dominance of the ideal of the "international man" reflects how the international secretariat was designed on the basis of a combination of legal and diplomatic skills. Discussing the process of state formation and the emergence of the bureaucratic field, Bourdieu argues that "it is necessary to understand the specific functioning of the bureaucratic microcosm and thus to analyze the genesis and structure of this universe of agents of the state who have constituted themselves into a state nobility by instituting the state, and in particular, by producing the performative discourse on the state which, under the guise of saying what the state is, caused the state to come into being by stating what it should be . . ." (1994, 16).

A similar dynamic can be found in the genesis of an international bureaucratic structure inasmuch as international civil servants constituted such a "microcosmos" that established a certain level of authority to define and act on some phenomena. They were not in a position to produce a "performative discourse" on the international. Rather, they worked with and through some member states to forge new categories and methods of operating that gave facticity to the idea of a rule-regulated international realm, where some types of skills were deemed important and useful for states. While the Secretariat was dominated by people with a legal background (Ranshofen-Wertheimer 1945, 405–6), there was a strong orientation toward the diplomatic skills seen to be key to managing the distinct environment of an international organization. Drummond (1931) emphasized, for example, that the international civil servant had "the capacity of placing [himself] in the position of the other man." Only through such an orientation, he argued, could the Secretariat "acquire the confidence of the fifty-four Governments whom it is their duty to serve *impartially* and to the best of their ability" (231; emphasis added). A "diplomatic" culture became central to the League Secretariat. Reflecting on his experience from the League, Egon Ranshofen-Wertheimer (1945) noted that

> there was in the Secretariat of the League of Nations a diplomatic or rather foreign office atmosphere. The daily routine of the officials necessitated contacts with diplomatic representatives and the permanent delegates accredited to the League. On missions at home or in other countries one of the first steps undertaken by officials was to get in touch with the foreign office. Moreover, a good deal of the social life of the official was diplomatic. (403)

The stress on impartiality, competence, and international loyalty together constituted "international capital"—a set of skills honed from the development and application of rules to regulate interstate affairs. None of this is to suggest that the League's Secretariat had any level of general authority over member states. Nonetheless, it is no coincidence that it is in this very same period that we see the emergence of discussions of an international community with a distinct legal identity. Referring to *jus cogens* norms and obligations *erga omnes*, Kratochwil notes that both were part of a "larger debate that reaches back to the years between the Firsts and Second World Wars," a debate that resulted in the establishment of a "notion of an *international community* as a subject endowed with rights—in the case of *erga omnes* obligations—and with some law-making capacities, as exemplified by *jus cogens*" (Kratochwil 2014, 152). Indeed, some sections of the League Secretariat did succeed in gaining recognition that arguably put them in a position of authority over particular tasks vis a vis member states. Under the directorship of Eric Colban, the Minorities Section engineered a series of practices—petitions, missions and bilateral meetings with governments— that placed the de facto responsibility for resolving the sensitive question of minorities with the Secretariat rather than member state representatives at the League Council or Assembly (Fink 2004, 274–83). It was Colban, for example, who negotiated directly with governments on how the League should handle minorities issues and who brokered the 1922 Geneva Convention between Germany and Poland (Ibid., 279). The protection of minorities here emerged not so much as a norm that the League was set to uphold as it was a delimited area of intervention that could demonstrate the League's relevance for the maintenance of the newly established international order at the Paris Peace Conference. Similarly, the work of the Permanent Mandates Commission (Pedersen 2007) inaugurated a series of practices that later became central to the UN's Trusteeship Council. When we now turn to the formation of the UN Secretariat, we will see how the initial construction of the international as a space for rule-based and impartial regulation and its associated cadre of international civil servants helped shape the form and role of the Secretariat to engage in "international rule."

The UN Secretariat: Institutionalizing International Capital

When state representatives met in San Francisco to negotiate the UN Charter, they continued in the League tradition, defining the Secretariat as a permanent, independent, and international civil service organization headed by a secretary-general. Article 100(1) states that the "Secretary-General and his staff shall not seek or receive instructions from any Government or from any other authority external to the Organization" and that they "shall refrain from any action which might reflect on their position as international officials responsible only to the Organization." Further, Article 101(3) states that competence and international loyalty trump national or geographic representation: "paramount consideration" is to be given to "securing the highest standards of efficiency, competence, and integrity" while geographical basis is to be given "due regard." Just as in the League, neither the Charter nor the preparatory work specified the skills or competence needed. International civil servants were thus to be distinguished from others by virtue first and foremost of their international loyalty and orientation. As one observer put it, "The most important characteristic of the international administration is that the staff must be completely interchangeable" so as to make it clear that nationality is irrelevant (Lengyel 1959, 520–21). The same observer pointed to the need for the nurturing of a truly international professional ethos: "No self-respecting profession is ever without [an ethos], and a profession as new as and exposed as the international civil service stands doubly in need of such a crutch to its own self-confidence" (525). Referring to the lack of a "common cultural background," another observer noted that an international civil service "has no such 'natural' basis on which to operate. It is essentially an institution derived from an exclusively rational recognition of the need for its existence." As such, it is a "fragile" structure, with relationships that are "diplomatic rather than administrative—diplomatic in that cooperation depends . . . on persistent recourse to the arts of persuasion [rather] than on continuous exercise of the power of command" (Winchmore 1965, 624). The defining "international loyalty" of this international civil service was also to be supported by economic incentives. The so-called Noblemaire principle, adopted from the days of the League and still in effect today, states that international civil servants shall be paid "favorably" compared to the highest-paid comparable national civil servants among UN members (UN 2004, 2–3). Moreover, it was decided that it was important to offer permanent contracts in an effort to ensure that staff would divest their national loyalties and become truly independent of their national governments for their future careers. The Preparatory Commission of the United Nations stated in this regard that "members of the staff [cannot] be expected fully to subordinate the special interests of their countries to the international interest if they are merely detached temporarily from national administrations and remain dependent upon them for their future" (quoted in Kay 1966, 64).

All of this suggests that the category of the international referred to a distinct realm to be regulated, however minimally, thereby requiring civil servants with an orientation and exclusive loyalty to this realm. The competence and authority of the secretary-general and of the Secretariat were nonetheless contested and precarious. Only a few years after its establishment, the independence of international civil service was being "threatened . . . by the continuing tension between international law and national sovereignty, but even more acutely by the depth of the cleavage and mutual suspicion between the communist and the anti-communist powers" (Friedmann 1952, 18). The reference here is to the formal competence of the Secretariat and of the secretary-general as its chief executive officer to challenge an investigation prompted by the US Senate into "subversive" activities of US nationals employed by the Secretariat. The tradition of having permanent contracts was also challenged from early on. The Soviet Union, for example, challenged the image of a national civil service on which the Secretariat model was based.

To regard the career civil service as the backbone of the Secretariat was to make the mistake of comparing the work and legal status of the United Nations Secretariat staff with the status of the civil servants of a state . . . the United Nations was a political organization, and all its organs, including the Secretariat, shared that political character. (quoted in Kay 1966, 66)

This intervention is nonetheless a testament to the relative success of the establishment of a category of the international civil service as impartial and independent—as holding a position of potential authority over the international—inasmuch as the Soviet representative did not challenge the Secretariat's existence but rather called for a marked reduction in permanent staff, suggesting instead a balance of 25–75 percent of permanent to fixed-term staff (Kay 1966, 66). The context of this criticism of the Secretariat was the fallout over Secretary-General Dag Hammarskjöld's handling of the Congo Crisis. Hammarskjöld had been instrumental in forging an expansion of the authority of the Secretariat during the Suez Crisis in 1956 that prompted the establishment of UN Emergency Force (Orford 2011). Prior to the Suez Crisis, Hammarskjöld had already established a level of authority independent from the explicit stipulations of the Charter by virtue of claiming to act as a representative of the international community, as distinct from the sum total of member states' interests.

Hammarskjöld and the Expansion of the UN Secretariat's Authority

There are no provisions in the UN Charter for what is today typically referred to as the "good offices" functions of the UN Secretariat and of the secretary-general. It implies an independent role as mediator and problem-solver. Writing in 1982, an observer of the role of the secretary-general and the Secretariat concluded that "the practice [of good office functions] is so extensive that it may be said that the competence of the Secretary-General to exercise good offices has concretized into a rule of customary law within the United Nations" (Ramcharan 1982, 136). The first and most significant instance of the invocation of such a role came when Secretary-General Hammarskjöld sought the release of US soldiers serving under the UN command in Korea who had been captured in China (Orford 2011, 43–46). It came to define the "Peking Formula." It meant "acting in his role as Secretary-General under the Charter of the United Nations and *not as a representative* of what was stated in the General Assembly resolution" and an explicit distancing from "undiplomatically formulated resolutions" by member states.[2] In so doing, Hammarskjöld effectively claimed a position of authority with basis in his interpretation of the UN Charter and the "international" responsibilities of the secretary-general, which was for *him* rather than member states to interpret and act on: it was a claim to representation that shifted the register from member states' instructions and to the contents of the UN Charter.

We are now in a better position to see how international organizations' authority—at least *this* particular international organization—does not flow from its bureaucratic features; even when and if it does, the link between authority and bureaucracy must be accounted for. In their seminal work on the authority of international organizations, Barnett and Finnemore (2004) note that "IOs are bureaucracies,"

> and bureaucracy is the embodiment of rational-legal authority. . . . Investing authority in bureaucracies has important consequences since bureaucracies make general, impersonal rules that order and classify the world. . . . The authority of IOs, and bureaucracies generally, . . . lies in their ability to present themselves as impersonal and neutral—as not exercising power but instead serving others. (21)

This is a highly potent description of the possible authority of IOs. To transform it into an *explanation* of such authority, however, the two key components must be separated and brought together under a different analytical framework. The first step is to explain how and why the UN Secretariat came to embody or be recognized as having "rational-legal authority." I have done so by linking it to the particular competition between lawyers and diplomats over the proper methods by which to regulate interstate affairs, resulting not in the dominance of international lawyers but in the recognition—over time—within diplomatic circles that a distinctively legally inspired "peace technique" was viable and was to be vested in an international organization with a permanent secretariat. There was thus a distinct legal rationality in the operations and ethos of the international civil servant as a new type of professional committed to things international.

But the existence of such a legal rationality within the Secretariat is not in itself an explanation of the Secretariat's authority. Hence a second step is needed: Barnett and Finnemore refer to the "ability to present themselves as impersonal and neutral—as not exercising power but instead serving others." This phrase contains an important insight that we can now unpack, but to do so, we need to make a detour via a discussion of the distinction between "in authority" and "an authority" (Friedman 1990). "In authority" is regulated by rules and procedures, the point being that the authority in question is independent of the qualifications and competence of the person holding office or being authorized by legal rules to undertake certain actions and to make others defer to his or her commands. It is, in this case, formalized in the UN Charter, stipulating the powers of the office of the secretary-general. "In authority" is therefore characterized by a mutual recognition among actors that they are equal yet not able to forge a common position: it is assumed that no one actor can persuade others on substance to substitute their own judgment for that of another actor. For this reason, an authority is set up and guided by rules to make binding decisions, where the authority of the decision is vested in the institution or office, not the person occupying it (80–83). "An authority," by contrast, presupposes precisely the opposite— namely, a recognition of inequality in that some actors are considered to have expertise, skills, experiences, or other attributes that make others defer judgment to the actor recognized as "an authority." There is another presupposition as well: for "an authority" to exist, there must be a *shared epistemological framework* within which it is possible to assess and judge who has more competence and skills and wisdom than others. A medical doctor, for example, is "an authority" because he or she can be judged to be more competent and knowledgeable than others within the register of a particular epistemological framework (83). The claim to authority that an actor makes is here not based on this actor's role or position, as in the case of an actor that is "in authority." Rather, the claim to authority is independent of procedural matters, vested in the capacities of the actor.

This should all be familiar, in that "in authority" is very similar to Weber's legal-rational authority, whereas an authority is perhaps best exemplified by his category of charismatic authority. The former is regulated by rules and adheres to—indeed, upholds—the established order. The latter carries the capacity to transcend this order. They rest on diametrically opposed social and political presuppositions that underwrite distinct types of authority that often go together in practice.

This distinction between in authority and an authority is helpful because it can help account for how international authority is established, institutionalized, and undone. The conflicting presuppositions of being in authority and an authority help us *see what was at stake* in Hammarskjöld's claims to represent the "international": Hammarskjöld expanded the authority of the Secretariat by virtue of claiming to represent the international, thereby bridging and concealing the contradictory presuppositions between his position as in authority and that of being an authority. In claiming—and succeeding—to represent the international, the secretary-general and the Secretariat appropriated authority that transcends the rules and procedures that are the legal basis for its authority. By presenting what is being done as being in keeping with established procedures to advance a mandate given by equally sovereign states—to present oneself "as not exercising power but instead serving others"—it is possible to establish a position of *an authority* that introduces *inequality*. (IOs are presented as *more* competent and skilled than others to define and advance things international.) This expansion of authority operated here through the advancement precisely of a concept of the international that is defined as empirically existing yet in need of identification and continual refinement by some especially skilled actors.

The authority claimed by Hammarskjöld was quite explicitly professed to flow from the text—or (depending on context) the broader spirit—of the UN Charter. But this claim to authority ultimately stemmed from the mobilization and production of the concept of the international—as distinct from and standing above the sum total of member states' particular interests. During the plenary session of the General Assembly in 1960, with the mission in Congo ongoing, Soviet premier Nikita Khrushchev attacked Hammarskjöld, saying not only that he should resign but that the whole post of secretary-general should be abolished, to be replaced by a troika representing the Eastern Bloc, the Western Bloc, and "neutral" countries. The Soviet premier said that Hammarskjöld, as chief executive of Congo operation, was aiding the "colonialists" in their efforts to

> secure the establishment of a puppet government, a government which, though ostensibly "independent," would in fact carry out the wishes of the colonialists. It is deplorable that they have been doing their dirty work in the Congo through the Secretary-General of the United Nations, and his staff. (Khrushchev 1960, paras. 141–42)

Hammarskjöld had, Khrushchev argued, "violated the elementary principles of justice in such an important post as that of the Secretary General" (Hammarskjöld 1960, para. 4). Hammarskjöld responded, "I shall remain in my post during the term of my office as a servant of the Organization in the interest of all those other nations, as long as they wish me to do so. In this context the representative of the Soviet Union spoke of courage. It is very easy to resign. It is not easy to stay on. It is very easy to bow to the wishes of a Big Power" (paras. 2–7).

This debate and Hammarskjöld's defense of the neutrality and impartiality of the Secretariat reveal something significant by highlighting how claims to representation were integral to the expansion of authority under Hammarskjöld. (Cf. Orford 2011.) In a speech delivered at Oxford University in May 1961, Hammarskjöld elaborated on his views on the nature and role of his office and that of the Secretariat. He started by citing an interview with Khrushchev reported by Walter Lippman in which the Soviet premier had reportedly said that "while there are neutral countries, there are no neutral men" and that consequently, "there can be no such thing as an impartial civil servant in this deeply divided world, and that the kind of political celibacy which the British theory of the civil servant calls for, is in international affairs a fiction" (Hammarskjöld 1961, 329).

Hammarskjöld proceeded to invoke a concept of the international as a distinct realm, as more than the mere relations between sovereign entities, to argue that such views on the role and work of the UN Secretariat

> challenged the basic tenets in the philosophy of both the League of Nations and the United Nations, as one of the essential points on which these experiments in international cooperation represent an advance beyond "conference diplomacy" is the introduction on the international arena of joint permanent organs, employing a neutral civil service. (329)

As already noted, this concept of the international was heavily shaped by ideas about the applicability of legal rules to this realm. It was also influenced by Hammarskjöld's own distinct position, owing to his professional trajectory and attendant disposition: Hammarskjöld had a law degree and came from a family of distinguished lawyers that had for a generation been engaged in the liberal cum political project of substituting diplomacy for the rule of law. His father, Hjalmar, was a former prime minister of Sweden, an expert on constitutional law, and a member of the Hague International Board of Arbitration. The secretary-general's brother, Åke, was registrar of the Permanent Court of International Justice. As a career civil servant in Sweden, Dag Hammarskjöld was well attuned to the limits of and opportunities for making the most of creative interpretations of legal categories. It is thus not surprising that, as Oscar Schachter (1962) notes,

> Hammarskjöld made no distinction between law and policy; in this he departed clearly from the prevailing positivist approach. He viewed

the body of law not merely as a technical set of rules and procedures, but as the *authoritative expression of principles* that determine the goals and direction of collective action." (2; emphasis added)

Hammarskjöld thus argued that the Charter—properly interpreted—sometimes required the secretary-general to act in defiance of some member states' views. Hammarskjöld's legal defense of his actions as secretary-general as being "neutral" and as well within the letter of the Charter, even in the face of opposition and harsh criticism of one veto power (the Soviet Union), was premised on an unspecified and therefore highly effective concept of the international. Of central importance here is how Hammarskjöld distinguished between an "intergovernmental" and an "international" secretariat. The former is a system in which member states together alternate to second and lend their services to the organization as a "bureau," with little or no independence. The latter, however, is a system in which an "international" civil service functions as an independent and neutral actor that is engaged in "executive action" on behalf of member states but somehow independent from those who delegated the authority to undertake such action. This neutrality could only be anchored in some higher principle, as it did not flow from the Charter itself. This higher principle was the concept of the international, latent with legal rules as an expression of an evolving public opinion about the need to prevent war and establish rules in the conduct of interstate affairs to be advanced by the Secretariat.

The claim to represent the *international* as a distinct space where some tasks were to be handled by the Secretariat gave the Secretariat and the secretary-general a level of authority vis a vis member states. Occupying a position "in authority," defined by the UN Charter, Hammarskjold, probably more than any other secretary-general, proceeded to speak and act as "an authority" on things international under the shield of merely doing what the UN Charter provided. In this context, it is significant how the secretary-general's role is described today: "Equal parts diplomat and advocate, civil servant and CEO, the secretary-general is a symbol of United Nations ideals and a spokesman for the interests of the world's peoples, in particular the poor and vulnerable among them."[3]

This description of the secretary-general as an "advocate" and as a "spokesperson for the interests of the world's people, in particular the poor and vulnerable among them" is nowhere to be found in the UN Charter. Rather, it has evolved in and through practice. This is also the case for the secretary-general's so-called "good offices" functions: As one commentator noted already three decades ago, "the practice is so extensive that it may be said that the competence of the secretary-general to exercise good offices has concretized into a rule of customary law within the United Nations. (Ramcharan 1982, 136). States treated the international as a residual category, where the UN Secretariat could smooth cooperation and facilitate inter-state debates about how to act. But by virtue of there being *some* modicum of rules, and *some* element of common purpose as set out in the preamble of the Charter, the Secretariat could speak of, and claim to represent, the international in a way that was not taken out of thin air—it had a level of social facticity that could anchor claims to representation. Therefore, when Hammarskjold took on the criticism from Kruchev, he did so within a social space that already contained states' recognition of the Secretariat, and of the secretary-general, as having authority over a certain set of tasks. Indeed, it is with reference to a social space thus defined that it becomes comparatively difficult for representatives of states, and comparatively easy for representatives of international organizations, to claim to represent the international as it transcends the particular interests of each member state.

Conclusion

The claim to represent the "international" helped constitute and bring coherence to the international as an object of governing in its own right. In that sense, the claim to represent the international has a performative effect: that which is claimed to be represented—a group of individuals, a region, or the international—emerges with its meaning and boundary through the claim of representation. Bourdieu (2004) draws attention to this mechanism when he argues,

> Authorized delegation is that which is capable of mobilizing the group which authorizes it, and thereby of manifesting the group as much for itself (by helping to maintain its morale and belief in itself) as for others. (41)

But here we must introduce a qualifier: a representative or spokesperson brings the group represented into a specific form through his or her statements we can grasp. But the character of the relationship between the representer and the represented depends on the type of authority claimed. The drive to define and act on things international as part and parcel of efforts to establish authority over it is therefore distinct: it is highly unlikely that such international authority would emerge were it not for states' perceived thinness or weakness of such authority. That is, because the international space over which the Secretariat claimed an element of authority was already organized into sovereign states—in accordance also with the UN Charter's Article 2(7) about noninterference on matters "essentially within the domestic jurisdiction" of states—the claim to authority was over what they arguably saw as a residual category. It was a claim to authority over a social space that was regarded by member states as initially negatively defined—it was whatever did not fall under states' domestic jurisdiction. But there was a distinct element of misrecognition here, for once the international was defined in terms of rules, the management and implementation of which were to fall to the UN Secretariat, it contained within itself the symbolic material to shift the meaning of the international away from what Simpson (2001) calls "charter liberalism," in which domestic jurisdiction prevails over international rules, and toward "anti-plural liberalism," which seeks to use these international rules to change the parameters for such domestic jurisdiction (cf. Jabri 2013). It is to the dynamics of this field of international rule that I now turn.

CHAPTER 3

Ethnographic Sagacity and International Rule

We are now in a position to explore how the claim to authority over the "international" as a space to be managed in a distinct way by the UN Secretariat has come to shape the type of rule that the Secretariat has established over this space. The most significant aspect of the contemporary work of the Secretariat is that of managing UN peace operations, or peacebuilding efforts.[1] I argue that peacebuilding is a semiautonomous field whose hierarchies and logic can be traced back to the category of the international in whose name the Secretariat has established its authority. I explore three aspects. First, I show the continuity between pre– and post–Cold War peacebuilding efforts, locating it in the role of the Secretariat in managing the UN's trusteeship system. The shift toward more explicitly liberal and comprehensive peacebuilding efforts is explained by the presentation of the Secretariat as a seemingly neutral and impartial representative of the international and how this status shields and helps legitimize the persistent alliance between the Secretariat and *some* (largely Western) states, which pushes the contents of the category of the international in a particular (liberal) direction. Second, I detail how the category of the international, by virtue of the position of authority of those claiming to represent it, defines the international as superordinate and the local as subordinate in peacebuilding efforts. The field's evaluative criterion, I argue, is inherently linked to this hierarchical ordering where the meaning of the "local" is derived from the preeminence of the international, pushing peacebuilders to compete for what Steinmetz (2008b) has called "ethnographic sagacity" and to seek recognition from peers and superiors for their ability to deploy local knowledge as a means to further "international rule." Third, I show how the hierarchical ordering between the international and the local is reflected in the relative positions of so-called civil affairs officers and political affairs officers, in the UN secretariat with the latter in a super-ordinate position. In all, I argue, that the type of rule associated with peace-building is inherently linked to the distinct type of authority established by the Secretariat and where the professional competence of the international civil servant is a blend of diplomacy and social engineering.

Trusteeship as International Rule

In his analysis of *Two Liberalisms*, Gerry Simpson (2001) argues that there is a tension between two different conceptions of the international community in international law. One is what he calls "charter liberalism," in which non-interference prevails, as stipulated in the UN Charter, and in which states are the actors that enjoy classical liberal principles of autonomy. The other is what he calls "liberal anti-pluralism," where the status of the state to enjoy autonomy is conditional on states being governed in keeping with liberal principles, thus opening up the possibility of various forms of interference to police behavior. If the former is the concept of the international initially used to construct a level of authority for the UN Secretariat, the latter is that which is arguably closer to present-day peacebuilding efforts, where a host of liberal norms and principles are part and parcel of the project of institutional and political transformation that peacebuilding entails. Simpson shows that there was considerable debate at the San Francisco conference over these two liberalisms but that the charter liberalism concept ultimately prevailed. The Charter's Article 2(7) is explicit on noninterference: "Nothing contained in the present Charter shall authorize the United Nations to intervene in matters which are essentially within the domestic jurisdiction of any state." What is striking, however, is that since its very inception, the UN has had a system for monitoring and judging member states' internal affairs in the form of the UN Trusteeship Council and the Division of Trusteeship Affairs in the Secretariat. A brief exposition of the role of the trusteeship system reveals the continuities with the League of Nations as discussed in chapter 2, and points forward to the "liberal anti-pluralism" that characterizes contemporary peacebuilding practices.

Writing in 1962, Harold K. Jacobson noted that "the passing of colonialism has . . . confronted the United Nations with new problems and tasks, as the Congo dramatically illustrates. Thus, an important chapter in the history of international organization is almost concluded, while another is just beginning" (37). The beginning to which Jacobson refers is that which we today often label *development, peacekeeping,* or both or what I refer to simply as *peacebuilding.* The continuity between the past in terms of the UN's role as an intermediary between colonial powers and those living in "non-self-governing territories" or "trustees" and present-day peacebuilding efforts is important, because it was through the early institutionalization of ways to collect and use information about people under the aegis of the trusteeship system that the parameters for the distinct practice of "international" rule became established (Anghie 2006; Bravo 1979). That is, at stake in the constitution of authority over the "international" as a distinct social space was not only that the Secretariat appropriated for itself a position as a representative and spokesperson for the "international" but also that a system for knowledge production and attendant governing techniques were established in keeping with this very same vision. This was most clearly expressed in the Division of Trusteeship Affairs: while UN peace operations, with the exception of the Congo operation in 1960, were largely focused on monitoring an armistice or peace agreement, the management of the trusteeship system implied that the Secretariat was intimately involved in monitoring and assessing "domestic" governance arrangements since its inception.

Ralph Bunche of the US was central in the negotiations over the trusteeship system at the San Francisco conference, and it was he who pushed for Trygve Lie to insist that the role of the Secretariat be markedly more expansive and not dependent on "administrative" (colonial) powers (Urquhart 1993, ch. 10). Bunche argued that Lie had to have the administrative powers to "to transmit to him the agreements they had made with the General Assembly," which implied "a political role—not just a conference servicing one—for the Secretariat and began a tradition of Secretariat activism on the subject of decolonization, something which many colonial powers were keen to see deferred. With Lie's support, Bunche worked . . . to establish a competent division on this issue and fashion the Trusteeship Council into a meaningful body" (Thant and Scott 2007, 19; Urquhart 1993, ch. 10). The process of decolonization that the Secretariat became responsible for facilitating was central to the subsequent formation of a much more robust UN Secretariat whose self-stylization as neutral, competent, and independent made it into a machinery for managing things well beyond the realm between states. As one commentator has put it,

International trusteeship [implies] the existence of an *active international body* capable of operating *between* Colonial Powers and peoples and consequently of narrowing the former's traditional jurisdiction.

Only the emergence of this *third-party* could give a concrete dimension to the otherwise elusive idea of international trusteeship. (Bravo 1979, 394; emphasis added)

The idea of a neutral and independent actor here emerges as central to the very system of governing between colonial powers on the one hand and their colonial subjects on the other. It is in this context no coincidence that one of the first forays into "executive action" was precisely to manage the consequences of granting of independence to former trusteeship and mandate territories, as in the case of the Congo operation in 1960. As such, the Secretariat started early on—before the end of the Cold War—to build up considerable capacity to organize missions to evaluate the state of affairs and to organize petitions made by subjects living under colonial systems. Moreover, the forerunner to the UN Development Programme, the Expanded Program on Technical Assistance, was a central mechanism for colonial powers to conform to the Charter in terms of seeking to "develop" territories under their control. This served to institutionalize a capacity and a claim to expertise, within the Secretariat, of a distinct type of international rule. There is, therefore, a continuous line from the UN Secretariat's role in managing the trusteeship system and present-day peacebuilding. As such, the introduction of more explicitly liberal principles as foundational for the concept of the international after the end of the Cold War was but a small step for the Secretariat. Put differently, the practice of advancing a liberal concept of the international—one that tilted toward what Simpson calls "antiplural liberalism"—was already quite well developed when the Security Council formulated mandates that were more explicitly oriented in that direction (Orford 2011). As one commentator has noted,

The Trusteeship Council supervised and observed plebiscites, referenda, and elections in non-self-governing territories moving towards independence. Some thirty plebiscites, referenda, and elections in non-self-governing territories were conducted under UN Trusteeship Council auspices between 1956 and 1990. (Joyner 2002, 157)

It fell to the Secretariat's Division of Trusteeship Affairs (later Department of Trusteeship Affairs) to organize and manage these efforts. "Building on its trusteeship experience," the same author notes, "a second phase saw the UN sponsoring plebiscites for elections that were designed to permit non-self-governing territories to select through a democratic process their own form of government" (Joyner 2002, 157). He notes that the UN Transition Assistance Group "introduced a new phase of UN involvement in electoral matters, as elections were incorporated into the UN's peacekeeping role" (157).

The genesis of peacebuilding qua international rule, therefore, is intimately linked to the building of a cadre of international civil servants experienced in managing transitions to independence and thus also being involved in a state's "internal affairs." The establishment of these practices, such as electoral monitoring and assistance aimed at democratic elections, gave materiality to those very categories of the international advanced by the Secretariat, thus giving them an appearance of second nature, shielding their genesis and implications for the overall direction and work of the Secretariat. As such, the practice of managing trusteeship affairs positioned the Secretariat as a misrecognized independent and neutral actor in that international civil servants—required to be loyal solely to the UN and thus to things international—were all committed to expand what constituted international rule and to increase their control over peacebuilding as a distinct task (cf. Abbott 1988).

In this context, the publication of UN secretary-general Boutros Boutros-Ghali's "An Agenda for Peace" (UN 1992) is noteworthy for how it came to shape future peacebuilding practices even in the face of opposition from key member states. Its ability to shape future policy despite such opposition is a testament to the authority of the Secretariat, but this authority must be understood not as bureaucratic or vested in expertise per se but as resulting from the particular configuration between the Secretariat and the (largely Western) states whose cooperation secured an evaluative criterion for peacebuilding with a clear interventionist and liberal agenda. The secretary-general's report argued that peacebuilding must include "advancing efforts to protect human rights"—indeed, it was held that a "requirement for solutions to these problems lies in commitment to human rights" and that "the time of absolute and exclusive sovereignty has passed" (paras. 55, 17, 18). The report also stressed, however, that "the authority of the United Nations system to act in this field would rest on the consensus that social peace is as important as strategic or political peace" (para. 59). China, Russia, and the nonaligned movement (NAM) were skeptical of possible interference in domestic affairs. Their statements at the time expressed support for the UN to engage in preventing conflicts and rebuilding societies emerging from them but stressed that the UN should never trump the principle of noninterference and that such involvement would have to be based on state consent. Foreign Minister Qian Qichen outlined China's position:

It is our consistent view that peace-keeping operations should strictly conform to the principles of the U.N. Charter. . . . No peace-keeping operations or humanitarian aid programs should be permitted to interfere in the internal affairs of any country, still less to use force and get embroiled in a conflict between the parties. (quoted in Fravel 1996, 1106)

The Soviet Union had since the late 1980s been much more supportive. MacFarlane and Schnabel (1994) note that the Gorbachev and Yeltsin periods were marked by a distinct internationalist thinking and a relative if cautious support for multilateral efforts: "The USSR co-operated actively in the design of United Nations forces for Namibia, Angola, Nicaragua, Mozambique, and Cambodia" (307). Nonetheless, the Soviet Union and later Russia also referenced the need to uphold the sanctity of noninterference in domestic affairs and to ground it on the consent of the parties to the conflict (307).

The same goes for countries within NAM, which were adamant that peacebuilding should not intervene in the domestic affairs of states. The Indonesian representative, reading a statement from the nonaligned movement on the supplement to the "Agenda for Peace" (UN 1995), stressed that the core principles of peacebuilding should be "strengthened": as those principles, he listed "the consent of the States involved; non-intervention in the internal affairs of States; impartiality; the non-use of force."

How then, could the Secretariat nonetheless push forward and advance ever more expansive policy documents detailing a range of governing tools that would make peacebuilding more intrusive? These actions can be explained not solely by the authority of the Secretariat over things international but by the particular configuration of the Secretariat and key (mostly Western) states: the UN is established on the basis of sovereign inequality misrecognized as equality not only because of the broad powers of the permanent members of the Security Council (the P5) but more specifically because of the differentiation between these permanent members of the Security Council. The so called P3 (US, UK, France) are differentiated from China and Russia in that established practice in the Security Council is that they are the "penholders"—the drafters of all major Security Council resolutions. Another source of difference is that under established practice, P3 nationals occupy the top three positions other than the secretary-general: the undersecretary-generals for the Department of Peacekeeping Operations (DPKO) (France), the Office for the Coordination of Humanitarian Affairs (OCHA) (UK), and the Department of Political Affairs (DPA) (US).

It is thus not so much the bureaucratic features of the Secretariat that explain its authority. Rather, it is the claim to representation of the international, advanced by international civil servants, that helps legitimize and shield the larger influence of some states on the thinking and operations of the Secretariat. This particular configuration of actors has produced a significant system of *symbolic resources* that leaves states as powerful as Russia and China as well as countries operating through the NAM with fewer resources with which to establish alternative conceptions of the international. These states have few recognized forms of capital that can be brought to bear on debates over the contents of the international and over international rule other than engaging in a different type of political maneuvering of blocking and hollowing out the proposals produced by the Secretariat. As also explored in chapter 2, Russia, for example, has rarely invested in the project of international rule to be performed by the Secretariat and consequently has little specific purchase on debates that center on how to advance the project of international rule. Russian representatives thus typically resist, stall, and introduce caveats, all the time implicitly recognizing the project of international rule advanced by others in the absence of any alternative conceptualization. Absent the profit gained by working with and through the Secretariat to present as universal what are particular interests, these states are more often left rhetorically cornered, with few avenues through which to forge alternative conceptions of international rule (Krebs and Jackson 2007).

In the General Assembly's Special Committee on Peace Operations, representatives of the Secretariat are typically taken to task for promoting a particular agenda without duly consulting states that are often critical of the peacebuilding agenda. Representatives from NAM countries charge that the DPKO is supporting the agenda of Western governments and that it consistently seeks to advance and expand the liberal register of peacebuilding. An Indian diplomat recalled the debate over the issue of "protection of civilians" as an integral part of peacebuilding efforts within the Special Committee in 2010: India and other NAM countries criticized the DPKO for presenting a policy paper on that issue when the committee had not asked for it. It had been pushed by Western states, and the DPKO had responded by producing a policy paper.[2] NAM countries argued that they contribute some 80 percent of troops to UN peacebuilding efforts and have a claim to place caveats on what their troops may and may not do. Deploying his nation's credentials as a major troop-contributing country, the Indian diplomat noted, "It is easy for Western governments to call for 'robust peacekeeping' and for seeking to strengthen efforts to protect civilians by UN troops, but it is our troops that may end up in harm's way."[3] Another diplomat from a NAM country noted that "the content was problematic for NAM—but it was the way issues were being developed and presented that annoyed them. No one had asked for a paper on 'robust peacekeeping.'" And the joint paper by DPKO and OCHA on protection of civilians was seen to be imposed on them. The same diplomat noted that "the Secretariat then backed up and tried to consult— and tried to give the impression of consultation," an indication of the quite considerable leeway of the Secretariat to push through its agenda by virtue not only of being the conveyer and producer of authoritative knowledge but also of its ties with and support from some states, such as France, the UK, and the US.[4] Representatives of Western states—occupying positions as recognized supporters and "friends" of the Secretariat in its push to advance peacebuilding—describe NAM's behavior as tending to "politicize" peacebuilding whereas they seek (simply) to "professionalize" peacebuilding efforts.[5] A Western diplomat referred to how NAM representatives "block progress" on peacebuilding by engaging in excessive "diplomatic games."[6]

This dynamic and the central position of the Secretariat as a producer of policy papers and best practices in keeping with a commitment to advance international rule explain how liberal principles were progressively made more important and defining for this international space over the 1990s and beyond. Thus, the categories with and through which peacebuilding is debated offer few available options for resistance and contestation on the substance of thickening the international space with more rules. Or rather, invoking sovereignty and noninterference in domestic affairs amounts to a concept of the international that is negatively defined, one that is bound to be resisted by international civil servants who are committed to international rule just as human rights lawyers are committed to human rights. It is no coincidence, given the legal component of the field's genesis, that there is a parallel here to lawyers' commitment to universality:

It is characteristic of the legal field generally that substantial value is typically assigned to those who reinforce the universal claims of law. Recognized high status within the legal field is given to those who help to build the universality that is essential to the legitimacy of law. (Dezalay and Garth 1996, 19)

While I agree with Orford (2011) that the establishment of the concept Responsibility to Protect is best understood as a move from deeds to words aimed at rationalizing the Secretariat's mode of international rule inaugurated under Hammarskjöld, the introduction of liberal principles as central to the concept of such international rule arguably did mark a shift in the register for peacebuilding: the significance of rights-endowed individuals became more important, leading to a shift from "juridical" to "empirical" sovereignty (Barnett 1995). This is expressed in the categories that structure the internal hierarchies and dynamics of the semiautonomous field of peacebuilding.

The International and the Local in the Field of Peacebuilding

Ralph Bunche was, as noted, a key architect of the UN Secretariat's Division of Trusteeship Affairs and was Hammarskjöld's most trusted adviser in the formative period of UN peacebuilding efforts. In his doctoral dissertation from Harvard in 1934, Bunche had observed that "Too often, . . . in the earnest consideration of Africa and her myriad problems, *sight is lost of the African*" (quoted in Robinson 2008, 4; emphasis added). As Hammarskjöld's envoy to the Congo during the Congo operation, Bunche sent a cable to UN headquarters on September 1, 1960. Referring to his negotiations with the Congolese government, he noted that

I . . . react very strongly against their endorsement of the thesis that there has been lack of consultation. Of course we can satisfy them by lip service to consultation even in cases where Govt. is utterly incompetent to judge or utterly incapable of acting but . . . the *ultimate responsibility must be ours* as we cannot, with open eyes, in order to placate Govt., do things we know to be harmful to best interests of the Congo. Indeed! (4; emphasis added)

By virtue of the authority that the UN Secretariat has established to engage in the management of crises and the task of keeping and building peace, its international civil servants are positioned as part diplomat, part social engineer, and the balancing of these two roles is key to the professional habitus of peacebuilders. Writing about diplomacy, Costas Constantinou (2013) has recently argued that

claims to diplomatic subjectivity aim to elevate one into an interlocutor whose separate will, interests, and ways of being deserve to be recognized as constituting "external" affairs. By contrast, the denial of diplomatic subjectivity reduces one into a subject of governance whose will, interests, and ways of being must be negotiated within the terms and parameters of "domestic" politics, sovereign authority, and the administration of populations. (142)

Such lack of diplomatic subjectivity is on display in how Bunche characterizes the Congolese government. It illustrates how Bunche as the representative of the "international" is not so much a mediator and neutral actor, positioned between states, but one with the skills and judgment on which some states depend for their progress. The position claimed by reference to the international in this way has an effect on that which in each specific case is to be acted on in the name of the international: governmental representatives of states that have a UN peacebuilding presence are thus typically not categorized within the register of diplomacy and "external affairs" but within the register of a hierarchical ordering where the international is the position from which judgments can be made about proper policy and behavior (Neumann and Sending 2010). The register of state fragility (Bhuta 2012) is but one example of this hierarchical ordering, where UN officials engage governmental representatives where the international is the frame of reference for the assessment of the local (Jabri 2013).

The ways in which the category of the international carries with it an implicit hierarchical ordering of states is also found in how the International Civil Service Commission (2013) describes the role and ideals of the international civil servant. The UN is said to "embody the highest aspirations of the peoples of the world"; "the international civil service bears responsibility for *translating these ideals into reality*"; and "over and above this, international civil servants have *a special calling*: to serve the ideals of peace, respect for fundamental rights, economic and social progress, and international cooperation" (3; emphasis added). Operating in a field whose social topography and positions are a product of the Secretariat's genesis in its engagement with member states (the international that it is to serve), not only are peacebuilders qua international civil servants "in" rather than "of" the local context in which they serve (Hopgood 2009), but their professionalism is seen to be based precisely on the maintenance of distance from this very local context.

Reflecting on his observations of the UN Transitional Authority in Cambodia (UNTAC), Amitav Ghosh (1994) notes that UNTAC staff

had no difficulty . . . in creating an absolute separation between itself and the society in which it was functioning: its boundaries were clear and self-evident. UNTAC employees and volunteers were foreigners, protected by a kind of diplomatic immunity, and distinguished by their appearance, their flags, and their cars: whatever their differences with each other, they were never so great as the difference between them and the general mass of Cambodians. (414)

My point here is that the precise meaning of the category of the "local," is derived from the position of authority claimed by representatives of the international and made manifest and embodied in the concrete practices through which peacebuilders operate. Ilana Feldman (2010) has documented how the UN Emergency Force (UNEF), established to secure withdrawal of Israeli troops from Gaza and Sinai, was organized to minimize "the kinds of contacts that its soldiers could have with the Gazan population" (422) and included cultural training and staff rules aimed to avoid having UNEF troops become "friends with Gazans," thus "protect[ing] UNEF's overall mission, and therefore the ideal of the international community that it represented" (423). It is no coincidence that the practices established to create a distance between those who represent and act in the name of the international and those who live in the particular—local—place where peace is to be built in many ways mirror the professional ethos of diplomats. Building on Sasson Sofer's (1997) argument about the diplomat as "stranger," Paul Sharp (2009) argues that diplomats

are examples of a particular kind of stranger. Like other strangers, they seek to become familiar with and to those with whom they have relations. Unlike them, however, they also work to maintain a distance. (99–100)

Peacebuilders qua international civil servants occupy a similar position in that their authority is claimed with reference to the international, which is to be defined in contrast to the local and particular. At the same time, peacebuilders are given a specific mandate to transform and thus to apply governance techniques—necessitating a move away from diplomatic subjectivity—to the societies in which they are operating. As such, peacebuilders also come equipped with lessons learned and best practices—codified by the UN Department of Peacekeeping Operations—that form the basis for how they seek to act on the societies in question and thus engage in what approximates social engineering. As a result, the field of peacebuilding thrives on how peacebuilders seek recognition from each other with reference to an evaluative criterion of how best to advance international rule by bringing to bear their view of the local as a means to facilitate the implementation of international standards.

International Rule and the Deployment of Local Knowledge as Capital

Peacebuilders seek to appropriate and demonstrate to peers and superiors their grasp of the local context but in a way that retains distance to make possible a translation of such insights that is compatible with the positions that they have as "internationals." For example, the Office of the High Commissioner on Human Rights (2006) discusses the rule of law in post-conflict settings by invoking an Archimedean, liberal position from which to assess it (see Bhuta 2008): "Understanding how the justice sector actually worked in the State before and during the conflict, and how it should function if the rule of law is to take root, should be a central feature of any peacekeeping operation" (1). The document proceeds to assert that "monitoring the administration of justice is also important as a way to test a Government's good faith and intentions" and that

> a government's true commitment to upholding judicial guarantees can best be determined by its willingness or refusal to implement legal reforms when the peacekeeping operation presents it with solid, substantiated information and recommendations, and feasible responses to the problem. (2–3)

Notwithstanding the legal-political authority conferred by international human rights law, these actors' dominance in defining the terms for peacebuilding efforts is arguably the result of a predominance of power on the part of some actors, but it is rationalized and presented—and (mis)recognized within the field—as inherent in the virtues and claimed universalism of liberal values and attendant strategies for their realization that is placed under the seemingly neutral category of the international. The classificatory schemes through which and with which all actors engage in the field as regards what peace is and how to advance it are rigged in favor of those who promote liberal principles as being foundational. The position of the international is here linked directly to a social engineering mode of operation inasmuch as it implies an image of politics as a "mechanism, to be calibrated, measured, engineered (*known*) and, ultimately, invented and designed" (Bhuta 2008, 517). It is reflected, for example, in the UN Peacebuilding Support Office's lessons learned on peacebuilding efforts. Based at UN headquarters, the office seeks to define peacebuilding in keeping with its position as a clearinghouse for best practices and thus to situate the local with reference to the international. It identifies a point outside society from which calibration of peacebuilding efforts should proceed:

> One of the main conclusions to emerge from the Working Group's review of comparative experiences in peacebuilding is that each case is unique. There are no universal lessons and no ready-made, "one-size-fits-all" models. Nonetheless, as highlighted in the different sessions of the Working Group, there are certain normative frameworks . . . which enjoy widespread acceptance. . . . The challenge, therefore, *lies in calibrating general principles with country-specific realities based on an accurate analysis of commonalities and differences among countries.* (UN 2008; emphasis added)

The recognition of having to avoid universalist templates operates from inside an understanding that holds peacebuilding as a practice of calibrating and adapting nonnegotiable general principles to knowledge of country-specific realities. It is the peacebuilders who are to "calibrate" the model to fit with "country-specific realities" based on their analysis of "commonalities and differences" between countries. Peacebuilders define ownership as theirs to give to national or local actors, depending on the extent to which local actors are deemed to have the necessary skills and "political will" (UN 2009, 5). But this Archimedean view should not be mistaken for a homogenous and omnipotent discourse, as if all those engaged in peacebuilding by necessity adopt such a view (cf. Autesserre 2010; Bhuta 2008). Rather, it is the evaluative criterion that defines the hierarchies within this field, where different actors, all of whom seek to demonstrate to others and receive recognition for their distinctive knowledge and interpretation of the local context as a means to advance and smooth the implementation of international rule.

Converting Ethnographic Capital to the Task of International Rule

In between two meetings on a field trip in Juba, South Sudan, in the fall of 2010, I was seated in the back of a Toyota Land Cruiser, listening to the conversation in the front seat between a former and a current UN official discussing the political situation in the country. They were talking about the upcoming referendum and the potential for conflict between Juba and Khartoum. The current UN official—working for the United Nations Mission in Sudan (UNMIS)—gave his reading of the situation, citing names of key people in the South Sudan People's Liberation Movement (SPLM/A) and their alliances and loyalties, and made predictions about what Salva Kiir, then first vice president of Sudan, would most likely do under different circumstances. The former UN official, who had finished a two-year stint at UNMIS in Juba the preceding year, responded by offering a different reading of the political scene. Invoking her knowledge of past SPLM/A decisions to which the other UN official had not been privy, she opined, "I don't think he's going to do that. Based on what he has said and done in the past, and his proximity to *A*, I think he will do *X*." The other UN official proceeded to cite several more recent decisions and events, mentioning alliances in South Sudanese politics, to suggest that his interpretation was the more plausible one. And so they discussed, over the course of the next ten minutes, how the political leadership of SPLM/A was likely to behave over the next few months.[7]

This conversation captures the prevailing form of capital and by implication what types of knowledge claims are recognized as authoritative, in the field of peacebuilding: peacebuilders—professionals of different backgrounds who work for the UN in either conflict or postconflict settings—compete with each other and seek recognition for their ability to offer nuanced and well-informed analyses of the political situation in which they work. This push to demonstrate what Steinmetz (2008b) has called "ethnographic sagacity" is reflected in the institutional practices of peacebuilding. They are organized around the advancement of a distinct form of rule that is bound up with—and endogenous to—the category of the international over which the UN Secretariat claims authority. That is, the stakes in the field of peacebuilding revolve very much around the production and circulation of knowledge of the "local" context as a product of the category of the international, where the "local" assumes its meaning and subordinate position as particular arena for efforts to implement ideals of the international. As such, the local is instrumentalized as a means to advance other ends. Put differently, our two interlocutors in Juba were discussing South Sudanese politics not as a separate or self-contained political space but as an international governance object.

Peacebuilders command military and financial power, coupled with expertise on everything from security sector reform and rule of law to economic governance and gender. Compared to the governance capacity and resources of governments emerging from conflict, it is not surprising that analysts of peacebuilding attribute causal powers and agency in shaping outcomes to peacebuilders rather than to local actors (Autesserre 2010; Barnett 2006;

Paris 2004). But the preponderance of economic and military resources in the hands of peacebuilders is fundamentally structured and mediated by the institution of sovereignty, forcing peacebuilders to seek to match their international expertise, their knowledge of universals, to the particular context in which they find themselves. Consequently, it is important to conceptualize the positions and particular type of capital that local political actors possess as they engage representative peacebuilders. A key feature of the institution of sovereignty is that it constitutes some actors "in authority"—as politically powerful by virtue of some predefined rules, even in the absence of governance capacity and economic and military resources. A national government, however weak and disrupted by a violent conflict, is designated by international law as the primary interlocutor for external actors (Krasner 2004). Sovereignty thus accords nominal political capital to representatives of governments where peacebuilding efforts take place because local political actors, while having little governance capacity as measured by the standards brought to bear by peacebuilders, command the ability to say no to and negotiate with external actors and to mobilize segments of society. This nominal political capital has the effect of forcing peacebuilders to try convert their different forms of capital (expertise coupled with material resources) so that it has bearing on the behavior of local political actors and their constituencies. Much like colonial administrators before them, peacebuilders must work with and through middlemen (Bain 2003; Mehta 1999). As Ann Swidler (2009) has argued,

> Despite donors' prestige and financial heft, they have more difficulty penetrating and altering local patterns of governance than one might expect. . . . [W]hat donor organizations offer is received (or seized) within a different social organization, where intended and actual effects differ. (197)

The efficacy of the material and symbolic resources (military troops, financial resources, mandates from the UN Security Council) of peacebuilders must therefore be analyzed in terms of the specific logic of the field of peacebuilding and the criterion of evaluation that prevails in it: Sovereignty exerts structural pressure on peacebuilders to understand and navigate the empirical particulars within which they are to set to advance predefined ends. Actors' preexisting skills and expertise have to be converted into claims that are recognized by others as having bearing on how and with whom to operate to advance peacebuilding efforts in a particular, local setting. This is where ethnographic sagacity becomes so important, for it emerges as a necessary component for the maneuvering for the advancement of the project of reshaping states as stable components of the international. While there is certainly a premium on technical expertise about human rights, security sector reform, and electoral and constitutional reform, the most highly valued species of capital is that which enables the tailoring of interventions and the process of implementing them to maximize changes of advancing predefined ends.

One informant described this in terms of what anthropologists call "dwelling" (Ingold 2000)—of how one gradually becomes "encapsulated" by the context in which one operates, living in a "bubble." The informant explained that this is a function of the practical challenges of doing one's job: "This has to do with the task you are set to do. Most people want to do their job well. To do so, you have to know who to operate with and how to do things."[8] Another described his job as being shaped by a "cross-pressure to advance a set of principles on the one hand and having to deal with often recalcitrant political leaders on the other."[9] Asked about what types of knowledge and information from the countries were most highly valued at mission headquarters, a former UNMIL officer with several years in different counties in Liberia noted that he received most praise when he relayed to superiors in Monrovia that he had now developed a "who's who" database in the county where he was stationed. He noted that he eventually "had a profile on all political actors—and headquarters was very impressed. You have to be very open, make contact, and use different sources. Eventually, this pays off."[10]

A wide range of expertise is harnessed to the task of peacebuilding, with considerable differences and tensions between the actors involved. Thus, the explanation for what peacebuilders are doing does not rest with homogeneity among them—they do not share a homogenous frame or a discourse—but with the shared interest in the stakes in the field, within which their interests are differentiated and reflecting different types of skills and resources deployed to seek recognition for the ability to know and operate in the particular setting. For example, force commanders assess and propose actions that run counter to those advanced by the humanitarian elements of a UN mission, each invoking their specific guidelines and experience: Interviewing a UNHCR official the day after an exercise in the protection of civilians run by UNMIS military contingents, the official had little praise to offer to the military: "These guys don't know what protection is."[11]

One expression of the preeminence of knowledge of the local political scene is found in how peacebuilders report to the United Nations Security Council (UNSC) on progress of mandate implementation. They are required to do so at regular intervals, and they represent the principal means of general communication with the UNSC. They are written by political affairs officers at mission headquarters and then "washed politically" by officials in DPKO in New York. These reports represent a particular form of reporting that indicates what the missions view as important and find it opportune and useful to include, and officials often use the documents to push for mandate extension or expansion to establish more leverage. These reports start with a section entitled either "Major Development" or "Political Situation" and are packed with references to concrete incidents, to individuals and their interests, and to likely developments. A representative excerpt from a report on UNMIL written just after the swearing-in of President Ellen Johnson Sirleaf opens with a detailed description of appointees to various posts, implying that UNMIL leaders perceive this information as essential:

> The nominations to Cabinet posts have not been without some controversy. On 11 February, the President announced the nomination of Frances Johnson-Morris, current Chairperson of the National Elections Commission and former Chief Justice, for the position of Minister of Justice, while James Fromayan, current co-Chairperson of the Commission, was nominated for the position of Chairperson of the Commission. In a press statement issued 12 February, the Congress for Democratic Change challenged those two nominations, claiming that the President was rewarding those nominees for ensuring her victory in the run-off presidential elections. Those nominations are currently under review by the Senate. (UN 2006)

Similarly, the report on UNMIL from February 2011 starts with a detailed analysis of the ongoing political game in Liberia in advance of the election, implying that this is important for the UNSC to know to appreciate what UNMIL is doing, why, and how it is performing against benchmarks:

> In August 2010, the legislature adopted a joint resolution proposing amendments to the election-related provisions of the 1986 Constitution. These amendments include changing the requirement of the electoral system from an absolute to a simple majority for all elections except for president and vice-president. . . . The Constitution requires that amendments be ratified in a referendum held at least a year after the legislature's action. After considerable discussion about the feasibility of holding the referendum before the 2011 elections, the National Elections Commission decided to schedule it for 23 August 2011. . . . Meanwhile, political parties continued to strategically position themselves for the elections. The Unity Party, led by the

President, finalized its merger with the Liberia Action Party and the Liberia Unification Party. (UN 2011)

The format for these reports suggests that knowledge of who's who, what their interests and agendas are, what their position is in the national political landscape, and so on is institutionalized as important and even the dominant register for how to know a postconflict country. It is similarly reflected in how peacebuilders reflect on their work. In Liberia, a political affairs officer at UNMIL described how he operated by noting that

> You ask a lot of people—Civil Affairs in UNMIL, people in the ministries, you talk a lot before you do anything. That's the best approach. Asking people in the ministries. Who's got what knowledge. What's discussed already in the cabinet. And so on. It's Political Affairs 101. In my position you have to know who's got knowledge. I have to know who would object if they were not included. You've got to tap into what people know.[12]

A similar view of how to work with people is expressed in how the head of the Rule of Law Office in UNMIL described how people would ask for advice about how to get things done in the judicial sector:

> People would come here to get information. When they come in— when they do work within justice area—they come and you tell them how to handle the ministry. If there are people in there that get things done and so on. Or, in the case of the judiciary, the chief justice is a very difficult man if you don't handle him in the right way. You have to understand his history and background to get him on board.[13]

The "local" is here of the utmost importance, but it is important in the context of an overarching project of international rule that pushes participants to demonstrate their competence on how to navigate in a political system to which they are strangers.

Civil Affairs versus Political Affairs: Converting the Local in Service of the International

The ways in which the "international" structures the hierarchy within the field of peacebuilding is nowhere more clearly expressed than in the relationship between professional categories of international civil servants. Those actors who occupy central positions in political affairs in missions and in the Office of Operations (OO) in DPKO in New York are generally regarded as the most influential ones, given their proximity to those who make decisions. There is a high degree of circulation between Political Affairs and those in the Office of the Special Representative of the Secretary-General (SRSG) in Missions and OO in DPKO.[14] OO is responsible for planning, coordination, analysis, and overall strategy development for missions. OO is the desk for peacebuilding efforts, and it owns the mission internally in the DPKO. Those working in the Office of Rule of Law and Security Institutions (OROLSI) do not regularly communicate with missions on overall strategy but offer technical advice—analyses of their area of expertise, such as security sector reform. There is a hierarchy among OROLSI and OO that is a testament to the structure of the field. The OO represents greater accumulation of the capital that matters in the field: its agents are "operators," having to know whom to ally with to get things through the system. It is no coincidence that, as one interviewee put it, those in Political Affairs and in SRSG are often recruited to the OO: "Many staff who end up at HQ in OO are identified and sucked up from either Political Affairs or O/SRSG roles in missions," Whereas OO offers "day to day support to mission strategy and reporting," OROLSI is said to "provide policy, resource mobilization, evaluation, training support and thematic expertise to support specialist units in missions" such as gender and civil affairs.[15] This hierarchy is perhaps best expressed in the relationship between Civil Affairs officers and Political Affairs officers.

For staff in missions, proximity to the SRSG is a central marker of authority and status. For staff at UN headquarters, proximity to the secretary-general's office and close contact with members of the UNSC is similarly a marker of status: it is measured by the proximity to the center of the "international." Civil Affairs, meanwhile, is comparatively marginal, with only a handful of staff at UN headquarters in New York but with an extensive network of staff working in local communities and with local governmental representatives. According to its own professional identity, Civil Affairs agents are "out there doing the job" with and through local counterparts but ranking below Political Affairs officers by virtue of their local and particular, setting as opposed to the international (represented by UN headquarters in New York).

Mission UN headquarters—under the management of the SRSG and located in the capital—is made up of different sections, including Human Rights, Security Sector, Political Affairs, and Civil Affairs. Political Affairs officers are generally charged with analyzing the overall political and security situation in the country and offering guidance and support to the SRSG. Those who work in the SRSG's office—normally a small team—often come from Political Affairs work and liaise closely with them. Civil Affairs was established in earnest in UN peace operations in the Balkans in the 1990s. It generally has a small presence in mission headquarters, as its work is organized around capacity building, follow up of project implementation, and being the UN's eyes and ears throughout the country. They are often posted in remote areas, in small—often one-person—teams to work with local and regional governments. They are tasked with regular reporting to mission headquarters (Schia 2015).

This structure is important for an appreciation of how different types of knowledge are produced and assessed by others in the UN system. The knowledge produced and used by Civil Affairs officers is typically more oriented to reporting on the local situation in which they operate, drawing on their local contacts and interaction with local counterparts. Political Affairs officers working out of mission headquarters are similarly intimately aware of—and compete with each other over—the most "local" knowledge, such as who's who and what is going on in parliament, in a particular political party, or in the cabinet.

The main difference between these two forms of local knowledge is that information provided by Political Affairs officers is tailored to the communication with UN headquarters in New York, while that of Civil Affairs officers is primarily used as background material for the former's reporting up the chain of command. The assessments and priorities advanced by Political Affairs officers, charged with analyzing the overall political situation, are thus often at loggerheads with those advanced by Civil Affairs officers, whose job it is to do local conflict resolution, to build local capacity throughout the territory, and to report on local political developments. Both desks produce "local" knowledge, but there is a premium on the type of knowledge that can help smooth the implementation of predefined programs as opposed to knowledge to be used to reflect on and possibly transform these programs. But the explanation for why the type of knowledge produced by Political Affairs officers prevails is incomplete without a more fine-grained analysis of the professional profiles and background of those who work in Political and Civil Affairs. There are distinct differences between Civil Affairs officers and Political Affairs officers in terms of background and professional profile.[16] To the extent that Political Affairs officers view themselves and are viewed by others in the system as the best and brightest, the hierarchy between the two different types of local knowledge is reflected in the status and background of those who work there.

While Civil Affairs employees are distributed evenly between Western and non-Western staff, Political Affairs profiles are mainly Western. Moreover, Political Affairs officers more often come from a private sector or business background than civil affairs officers. One-third of the Political Affairs profiles mention a private sector job, compared to 7.7 percent of the Civil Affairs profiles. Conversely, while 52.0 percent of the Civil Affairs profiles list NGO employment, only 7.4 percent of the Political Affairs profiles present a NGO background. It is more common for Political Affairs officers to have listed a previous fast-track program within the UN system: 33 percent of the Political Affairs officers have a fast-track background, compared to 3.8 percent of the Civil Affairs profiles. Finally, crossovers between Political and Civil Affairs are rare, suggesting that these are distinct career trajectories.

TABLE 1. Political Affairs and Civil Affairs Officers Backgrounds and Profiles in Percentages

Nationality	Political Affairs	Civil Affairs	Total
Western Nationals	80.8	50.0	34.6
Non-Western Nationals	19.2	50.0	65.4
N = 53 (Valid 52)			
Private sector background			
Private sector	33.3	7.7	20.8
No private sector	66.7	92.3	79.2
N = 53 (Valid 53)			
NGO background			
NGO background	7.4	52.0	28.8
No NGO background	92.6	48.0	71.2
N = 53 (Valid 52)			
Fast-track programs			
Fast-track	33.3	3.8	18.9
No fast-track	66.7	96.2	81.1
N = 53 (Valid 53)			
Crossover			
Crossover	11.1	7.7	9.4
No Crossover	88.9	92.3	91.6
N = 53 (Valid 53)			

These positions shape how different types of local knowledge are seen as relevant for the task of building peace: Political Affairs and Civil Affairs officers' respective position-takings produce different and often competing views on how to define and act on particular situations, but Political Affairs officers, who are closer to the SRSG and thus the standards of the international that serve as the field's criterion of evaluation, typically prevail. UN Civil Affairs officers, whose job it is to be engaged in local conflict resolution and capacity building of local government throughout a country, see their counterparts in mission headquarters as insufficiently attentive to local conflict dynamics, and those stationed at mission headquarters regard those who work in local communities far removed from headquarters as missing the larger political picture. A former UNMIL Civil Affairs officer recounted how over the course of almost eight years in remote locations throughout Liberia, he constantly fought with colleagues and superiors in Monrovia for inclusion of specific mention and examples of violence and human rights violations to "remind them that we are talking about real people."[17] Another Civil Affairs officer noted that the "difference is that we in Civil Affairs have direct link with Liberians out in the county. In Monrovia, you interact mostly with other UN staff and with host government."[18] Indeed, Civil Affairs officers often function as spokespersons for local authorities vis-à-vis the national government. A former Civil Affairs Officer in UNMIL noted that

> there is always some tension between local authorities and the central government. National interests do not coincide with local interest. This is where Civil Affairs has a function. They report to headquarters on what are local issues. Sometimes, they cannot find voice through national media, so Civil Affairs become spokesperson for local issues.[19]

This tendency of peacebuilders to identify with and become spokespersons for local constituencies pervades peacebuilding efforts and can also take the form of tensions inside UN missions. In UNMIS, there was tension between those posted in Khartoum and those posted in Juba that reflects the competition over what type of local knowledge is to prevail in the advancement of international rule. Prior to South Sudan's independence, the government of Sudan had demanded that UNMIS headquarters be located in Khartoum and that decisions should be made there. A former UNMIS officer described this tendency on the part of UN staff to "go native" in the eyes of their colleagues stationed elsewhere. She described in detail the conflict between UNMIS in Khartoum and UNMIS in Juba: "Those in the

North thought we were too close to SPLA. We thought they were too close to and apologetic vis-à-vis the regime in Khartoum."[20]

Conclusion

The genesis of the category of the international is central to the constitution of peacebuilding: I have tried to show that peacebuilding is a field whose typography and stakes can be traced to the search for recognition and competition for authority both between the Secretariat and member states, and between different professional groups within the Secretariat. As such, I have tried to show that how the contents of a governance object and the practices established to govern it are endogenous to the initial search for and competition over a position of authority to control that object of governance (Abbott 2005). The effort to construct or define a governance object and to construct in a way that reflects and reinforces the preexisting capital or skills of particular actors in the ongoing competition for authority also extends to academic knowledge production.

I have made no claims to explain or account for peacebuilding outcomes in a particular country, limiting myself instead to an exploration of peacebuilding as a form of rule whose genesis is central to understanding its contemporary form. The field of peacebuilding is characterized by a privileging of and commitment to the international, but recognition as competent and even authoritative rests fundamentally on the ability to build up ethnographic capital and to bring that to bear on ways to calibrate and adapt the strategy to further international goals. In his writings on British colonial rule in India, Bernard Cohn (1996) notes that "knowledge of the history and practices of Indian states was seen as the most valuable form of knowledge on which to build the colonial state" (5). Present-day peacebuilding is similarly structured by peacebuilders'[21] search for recognition from peers in terms of knowing the local political scene, and this knowledge is essential to furthering a predefined set of liberal ends of peacebuilding (cf. Steinmetz 2008b). But there is a significant difference: colonial rule was premised on a "rule of difference" (Chatterjee 1993). It was justified for European publics with reference to the inferiority and thus also incapacity for self-government on the part of the colonized. Present-day peacebuilding is constituted by an explicit commitment to two potentially contradictory principles, liberalism and sovereignty. Whereas the former contain claims about universalism in order to justify efforts to bring about latent liberal principles everywhere (Hindess 2004), the latter contain rules to safeguard the particular.

The field of peacebuilding is only semiautonomous and heterodox—its functioning is shaped not only by the position of the UN Security Council, which provides mandates and thus intervenes in its functioning, but also by the tension between the realm of legitimation or justification and the realm of application. The realm of justification works on a presumed lack of hierarchy and difference—the same principles and rules are to apply everywhere—particularly so for an organization like the UN. At the same time, the particulars of each specific realm of application contradict this very presumption of universalism: while liberal ends are dominant, their implementation in any specific setting engenders a dynamic whereby peacebuilders are compelled to seek recognition for their ability to know the local political scene, because tailoring to the local context improves chances of some level of observable outcome that is believed to advance the liberal principles that peacebuilding practice is to advance. This duality of the field—anchored with reference both to an Archimedean position that is by definition detached from time and space and to the time- and space-specific setting where liberal principles are to be made manifest—reflects a particularly strong expression of a generic feature of any field of global governance. While liberal ends are orthodox, their implementation, as we have seen, generates a competition over local skills and networks to use as a tool to smooth the implementation of predefined project. As such, the premium placed on the translation from the universal to the particular and the instrumentalization of knowledge of the particular as a means to implement universals reflect the hierarchy between Political Affairs officers and Civil Affairs officers. And in that sense, the international is one sense a misrecognized placeholder—frame of reference—for the relative marginalization of the local qua an expression of the limits or outside of the UN Secretariat's legally inspired and rule-based claims to authority.

PART III

CHAPTER 4

Genesis of the Field of Transnational Population Governance

This chapter accounts for the genesis, social topography, and boundaries of the field of population governance, a field organized around a goal of population control that emerged as a transnational one from the late 1950s onward. In contrast to the two preceding chapters, this and the next chapter are about transnational rather than international authority. The distinction is an important one, for international authority involves the authority to define and operate in the realm between states. Transnational authority, by contrast, concerns governing projects that span different polities (states), where, as in the case to be analyzed here, actors in some countries are engaged in and are recognized as authorities on governing in other countries.

The analysis aims to demonstrate two main points. First, that in order to explain why an actor is recognized in a position of authority, it is necessary to explore the relations between a myriad of actors and the resources—material and symbolic—that these bring to bear as they vie for positions of authority. Second, how the classificatory struggles at stake in the competition for authority shape the hierarchies within and boundaries of a field over time. In short, not only are classification struggles part of the competition to become recognized as occupying a position of authority, the effects on the field of such struggles in terms of what becomes a field's symbolic capital (evaluative criterion) is crucial for an account of the future political dynamics of a field.

The Birth of Transnational Population Governance

Those who labeled themselves "population specialists" in the early years of the twentieth century were concerned with a range of issues, including "overpopulation, depopulation, uncontrolled fertility, excessively controlled fertility, unrestricted immigration, race suicide and race degradation" (Hodgson 1991, 1; see also Caldwell and Caldwell 1986; Kevles 1985; Reed 1978). The founding of the Population Association of America in 1931 served to establish an arena for competition between various groups over the authoritative definition of *population* as an object of governance, but it would take another two decades before these groups converge around a specific conception, crystallized in the theory of demographic transition, with population seen as intimately related to economic growth, development, and the defense of US interests against the threat of communism.

The actors that made up the protofield of population all shared an interest in the governance of fertility behavior in some form and advocated the establishment of conscious efforts to limit, space, and fine-tune fertility behavior, depending on race, socioeconomic class, and nation. Four groups defined the core of the still-unsettled field of population in the 1930s and 1940s, all differing markedly in their views on how and why to regulate fertility behavior: there were birth control advocates, Malthusians, eugenicists, and demographers. Identifying their forms of capital, conceptions of population governance, and their efforts to gain recognition from relevant others provides the raw material from which we can formulate an explanation for why one particular group—demographers at the Office for Population Research at Princeton University—emerged as authoritative and in a position to impose their theoretical formulation, the theory of demographic transition, as the very framework within which to think about and act on population issues.

Margaret Sanger had initiated the birth control movement in the US through public advocacy against the Comstock Law[1] and for the establishment of birth control clinics. Since the 1920s, she had traveled extensively to other countries, primarily in Europe and Asia, arguing the case for birth control as a matter of women's health and rights. Her writings, public advocacy, and travels were central to the establishment of national constituencies for fertility regulation that formed the platform, from the late 1950s onward, for population-control measures in India and elsewhere. Sanger's position was marked first and foremost by her own social capital: she met with political elites and population scientists of varying stripes in the US, the UK, India, and Japan and "could draw on a variety of political currencies based on social connections, professional credentials, and public notoriety" (Connelly 2008, 52; see also McCann 1994).

Birth controllers were chiefly concerned with individual women's access to means for controlling fertility. Spearheaded by Sanger in the US, by

Marie Stopes in the UK, and by Elise Ottosen Jensen in Scandinavia, they allied with eugenicists and Malthusians in an effort to convince skeptical publics of the importance of women's access to medical services pertaining to reproduction. It was Sanger who was instrumental in establishing both the Population Association of America and the International Union for the Scientific Study of Population. The core element of Sanger's strategy was to organize conferences where "notable" actors could discuss the means of and rationale for birth control—often with a strong eugenicist flavor. From the perspective of Sanger and her allies, these efforts were aimed precisely at recognition from actors with academic credentials. A signal achievement was the organization of a conference in New York in 1925 attended by John Maynard Keynes as well as other luminaries. As expressed by eugenicist Raymond Pearl, by organizing this conference, the birth controllers achieved a "certain academic degree of respectability" (quoted in Connelly 2008, 64; see also Reed 1978).

Malthusians saw population growth as a cause of hunger, depletion of national resources, international tensions, and war. Eugenicists, for their part, were concerned with the deteriorating "quality" of populations caused by the unchecked fertility of certain ethnic groups and lower socioeconomic classes. In discussions of interstate relations, eugenicists saw "race wars" as a real threat. The positions of both these groups owed much to the academic credentials of their members. For example, Charles Davenport, Raymond Pearl, and Henry Pratt Fairchild all espoused eugenicist views from university positions. Then there was the Malthusian Hugh Moore, who had made a fortune from his Dixie Cup Corporation and used the money to distribute his book, *The Population Bomb* (1954), and to fund other efforts. Frederick Osborn, a key entrepreneur in the field, espoused eugenicist views from both "pedigree and social position," operating from his position as head of the New York Zoological Museum. William Vogt could not boast of such pedigrees, but he was no less important in popularizing ideas about population growth: his 1948 book, *Road to Survival*, was translated into nine languages and became an international best seller (Connelly 2008, 128).

As for the members of the fourth group, the demographers, they were primarily intent on showcasing their skills by conducting social scientific analyses of relevance to the broader public. The Milbank Memorial Fund (MMF) had long been conducting research in the field of public health. In the 1920s, Edgar Sydenstricker, a public health researcher with a background in economics, initiated a range of studies of differential fertility rates between various socioeconomic and ethnic groups. The issue of differential fertility rates was a central part of the eugenics debate as to whether efforts in public health were merely keeping the "unfit" alive (Wiehl 1971, 63). Given the public health tradition within which this research was undertaken under Sydenstricker's supervision, identifying the specific causal factors that could explain these fertility differentials was pivotal. If these fertility rates could be explained sociologically, the provision of birth control methods could form part of the expanded public health agenda advocated by Sydenstricker and others at the MMF. As Frank Boudreau of the MMF noted, "It was decided to secure data on the prevalence and effectiveness of contraceptive methods in a number of different groups, and to learn, if possible, what effect contraception had on health" (Boudreau 1941, 40).

As Clyde Kiser (1971), who worked at the fund as a researcher beginning in 1931, recollected, "Mr. Kingsbury regarded birth control as something desirable from the standpoint of social welfare. Mr. Cochran, an economist, was much concerned about the problem of unemployment during the Depression" (20). It was a field-specific move inasmuch as the focus of research was structured by the actors' positions and views relative to biological explanations of fertility differentials. And in the context of New Deal efforts at handling problems of family health and welfare during the Great Depression, it was designed to demonstrate how social science analysis could contribute to the formulation of better public policy.

These four groups could be seen as constituting several different epistemic communities or an advocacy network, since they advanced arguments that all had some backing in scientifically produced knowledge that they had themselves been involved in producing. All four groups shared an interest in the regulation or control of reproduction. However, an explanation organized around either epistemic community or an advocacy network would misinterpret what was a shared interest in an issue for actual consensus on how to define and govern it.

Moreover, as Matthew Connelly (2008) shows in detail in his comprehensive account of the history of efforts to curb population growth, there were a myriad of family planning associations, eugenicist societies, Malthusians, and demographers in India, China, Japan, and elsewhere at this time. He notes, for example, that the fusion of birth controllers and eugenicists might very well have prevailed, judging by their strength in the 1920s and 1930s, in which case the methods to be used to regulate fertility and the justification for such regulation would have looked different. Indeed, even labeling these varied actors as distinct "groups" is problematic, as it fails to do justice to their varying configurations and outlooks over time as they contended for positions and access to resources with which to establish governance efforts.

When I highlight the heterogeneity of views about population in this way, it is because I want to capture their relations with each other in the quest for recognition in what increasingly came to look like a (proto)field: they cooperated, debated, and competed over status and over influence on how to define and seek to govern fertility behavior. These groups shared a concept of population but had different conceptions of how to define and govern it. And as much as these groups engaged with each other, they sought recognition for their own particular views and positions—by engaging in networking and public advocacy (birth controllers), by investing in research projects aimed at showcasing some causes as more relevant than others (demographers), by using prestigious university positions as a platform from which to call for increased "population quality" (eugenicists), or by warning the public of the advent of war and famine unless population control could be established (Malthusians). Before proceeding to account for why demographers associated with the Milbank Memorial Fund and later Princeton's Office of Population Research emerged in a position of authority relative to the other three groups, I should stress that scientifically produced knowledge, as conceived here, constitutes "capital" in Bourdieu's sense only in the context of the evaluative criterion of this particular field. It is an empirical question whether academic credentials matter or not, depending on how a field is constituted and differentiated from its environment.

In the case of population, two factors stand out as central in accounting for the status of scientifically produced knowledge. First, the moral, religious, and political sensitivities that characterized (and still characterize) questions of fertility regulation (contraceptive use, abortion, and so on) made scientific validation central to efforts to "sanitize" the call to political action. Since the very beginning, birth controllers had sought out alliances with scientific disciplines, including biology and medicine, in an effort to shift the focus away from the public and (in their eyes) politicized debate and into arenas where scientific knowledge could be harnessed to their cause. As Frank Notestein (1982), a key figure in the field of population, argued, "Probably the best way to make progress in a dangerous field is to sponsor 'research' rather than 'action.' . . . Keep clear of advocacy. So research becomes a substitute for action" (684; Reed 1978).

Second, the study of population dynamics had no institutional home in the university system in the first decades of the twentieth century. According to Greenhalgh (1996), students of population dynamics "lacked status, security and access to regular funding" compared to other scientific disciplines (30), so they looked outside the academic community for recognition and financial support. Pascal Whelpton (1954), another key demographer, stressed that research on population dynamics and fertility behavior was not geared principally toward "adding to scientific knowledge, but rather providing information and results that will be of use in the underdeveloped country or countries that we are considering" (139).

Thus, scientifically produced knowledge constituted a significant symbolic resource for engaging in classificatory struggles, but it was nonetheless recognition from policymakers or actors with resources to help initiate action programs that came to serve as the central criterion in determining which knowledge claims became authoritative.[2] Paradoxically, therefore, while scientifically produced knowledge was essential for claims to authority on what, how, and why to govern, it was recognition from actors outside academia—in business and politics, with resources that could help fund governance efforts—that proved essential in the adjudication between competing knowledge claims.

The Stakes of Classification: The Genesis and Contents of Transition Theory

In 1936, Frederick Osborn, former secretary of the American Eugenics Society, persuaded Princeton University and the MMF to establish an Office for Population Research (OPR). It was here that the same group of researchers who had been studying differential fertility rates to improve US public health efforts would formulate the theory of demographic transition during the 1940s. In Britain, Alexander Carr-Saunders' *The Population Problem* (1922) had identified some of the mechanisms that were to attract far greater interest from the early 1940s onward. And in the United States, Warren Thompson had as early as 1929 produced a theoretical formulation on the general historical relationship between population growth and economic growth that was strikingly similar to the theory of demographic transition. However, neither had any significant uptake, which calls for an account of the field-specific position and strategies that the formulators of transition theory employed in order to make it dominant (Szreter 1993, 664). The formulators of transition theory first wrote and then rewrote their theory, in a field-specific move to seek recognition not from peers in other academic disciplines but from actors with the resources to make programs possible.

Transition theory was formulated on the basis of empirics from two sets of studies, one commissioned by the League of Nations' Transit Department (housed at Princeton University), and the other commissioned by the Cartography Division of the US State Department. Both studies had the generic aim of including demographic data in planning for a post–World War II international organization and for future US foreign policy. Frank Notestein, Irene Tauber, and their colleagues at the OPR used the empirical data from these studies of population changes in Europe and Asia as the basis for their conceptualization of the demographic transition. Referring to global population growth since the seventeenth century, Notestein (1945) wrote, "The whole process of modernization in Europe and Europe overseas [colonies] brought rising levels of living, new controls over disease, and reduced mortality" (39). However, he subsequently pointed out, while the process of modernization quickly reduces mortality rates thanks to improved health conditions and welfare, fertility behavior changes far more slowly because various cultural and socioeconomic norms related to fertility are perpetuated (Notestein 1945, 40).

In the words of another key formulator of transition theory, Kingsley Davis (1944), "The rapid growth associated with the transition arises from a striking fact—namely, that in the transformation the death rate generally declines before the birth rate" (42–43). Thus, according to transition theory, the process of modernization necessarily leads to high population growth rates in the "transitional" period when mortality has declined but when fertility has yet to change in response to modernization (Davis 1944). Transition theory thus effectively transformed fertility behavior from a national phenomenon to be studied along the lines of socioeconomic class and the health and economic welfare of the family—which had been a mainstay among demographers, public health researchers, and economists for decades—to a global and historical phenomenon categorized by degree of "development" at the national level.

Crucially, this conceptual aggregation effectuated a break with the broader view of public health that had prevailed in nationally oriented studies by identifying a potential for high population growth rates in colonial areas in part precisely because colonial rulers had invested heavily in public-health-based interventions to control epidemics, thereby further widening the gap between mortality rates and fertility rates. In short, public health efforts were recognized as integral to the "imbalanced modernization" that was generating population growth (Davis 1944, 56–57; Notestein 1945, 50–51).

It is a testament to the search for recognition from policymakers that the first version of transition theory was presented at Hot Springs, Virginia, in 1943 to a conference of planners and policy administrators of the envisioned Food and Agricultural Organization of the United Nations (Schultz 1945). As originally formulated, transition theory described the causes and dynamics of population changes with reference to the process of modernization. It provided policy planners with a map of likely population trends in different world regions—without, however, offering explicit recommendations as to whether or how population growth could be acted on or deliberately governed. This was because fertility behavior was a dependent variable: fertility behavior, it was assumed, would change slowly in response to the socioeconomic and then cultural changes associated with the process of modernization (see Hodgson 1988; Szreter 1993).

By the late 1940s, Malthusians had helped establish a sense of urgency with the "population problem." Examples include William Vogt's (1948) *Road to Survival* and Fairfield Osborn's (1948/1968) *Our Plundered Planet*, both aimed at convincing the public that dramatic measures were needed and gaining recognition within the field for their particular reading of why and how to govern population dynamics. These analyses were marked not so much by scientific rigor as by graphic arguments about the many possible effects and perils of population growth.[3] Vogt (1948) argued that prewar Japan, "unwilling or not wise enough to seek a sharp limitation of her population, was faced with the dilemma: starve or fight"; he went on to say, "If the United States had spent two billion dollars developing . . . a contraceptive, instead of the atomic bomb, it would have contributed far more to our national security" (42, 146–51, cited in Critchlow 1999). The proclamation of the People's Republic of China in October 1949 constituted a major strategic challenge to US foreign policy. As viewed from Washington, DC, the fall of Chiang Kai-shek indicated the possibility of a "domino effect," with other countries following suit and adopting communist ideology (Szreter 1993, 675–76).

Social scientific analyses that could offer solutions to such a strategic challenge were thus in high demand (see Cooper and Packard 1997). India and Japan were already considered prime examples of the problems of high population growth, and the prospects of a communist domino effect in Asia served to put a high premium on efforts that the US could conceivably undertake to stall communist influence. But here the formulators of transition theory had no policy options to offer. High population growth rates were recognized as an obstacle to economic growth and development, yet the very solution to the problem of population growth offered by transition theory was to invest in economic development and societal "modernization" (Hodgson 1988, 547–48). The formulators of transition theory now proceeded to reverse the arrow of causality, in an explicit move to seek recognition from policymakers for their policy relevance.

Their first move was to redefine the term *demographic transition* from a theoretical formulation for grasping a complex set of socioeconomic and demographic changes to a definitive empirical description of a universal process (Szreter 1996). This loosening up of the conceptual structure of transition theory enabled these demographers to initiate a new line of reasoning: Notestein (1947), for example, now asserted that "there is nothing inevitable about the exact amount of time . . . involved in the demographic transition. Careful planning, particularly in the early stages, might speed up the process" (250). The motivation for this reformulation is clearly brought out by Notestein's (1947) assertion that "the problem [of high population growth] is too urgent to permit us to await the results of gradual processes of urbanization, such as took place in the Western world" (1947, 250; see also Szreter 1993, 671). And so he soon came to argue that "economic development needs to be accompanied by *explicit efforts to reduce fertility* in the world's major industrially underdeveloped but densely settled areas" (1950, 89).

Later, in 1950, the Rockefeller Foundation—by then a major financial supporter of research on population-related issues domestically—published a report that followed the same line of reasoning. Authored by Marshall Balfour, Roger Evans, Notestein, and Tauber (1950), the report held that "the problem of reducing the fertility of peasant populations has two parts, one relating to motives and the other to means" (118). Further, both means and motives "are amenable to attack and neither has received the attention it deserves" (118). Noting the lack of effective, easy-to-use methods of contraception, the report stressed that investment in research on the physiology of reproduction aimed at producing better means of contraception was a challenge that "could be attacked immediately in the West. We doubt that any other work offers a better opportunity for contributing to Asia's and the world's fundamental problems of human welfare" (120). In reformulating transition theory in this way, a tension emerged between the economic and health rationales that had originally been seen as mutually supportive: public health efforts emerged within the reformulated version of transition theory as integral to the problem of the "imbalanced modernization" that generated population growth (Notestein 1945, 50–51; see also Davis 1944, 56–57). Indeed, health considerations now emerged as part of the problem of high population growth in the developing world (because lower mortality rates were not accompanied by lower fertility rates).

This reformulated version of transition theory also postulated that it was possible and indeed advisable to work to control fertility, with two overarching strategies presenting themselves: developing and supplying contraceptive means for fertility regulation and seeking to change motivations. These two strategies pointed in very different directions: either invest in socioeconomic development, education, and public information to change motivation (demand-side approach) or develop and provide new and better contraceptives (supply-side approach). The supply-side approach prevailed, not only because it seemed to represent a relatively inexpensive and technological solution to a large-scale structural problem but also because investment in demand-side interventions would place efforts to control population growth within the context of already established efforts to spur economic development. The tensions between economic and health approaches and between means and motives were effects of the classificatory reengineering performed by the formulators of transition theory. This was to have central significance for the *nomos* of the field in terms of its autonomous logic and the boundaries drawn to adjacent fields, as will be explored in chapter 5.

Settling the Field: Economic Capital Meets Cultural Capital

Because of the premium placed on scientific knowledge (cultural capital) as a tool for galvanizing support for action, the researchers associated with the OPR were recognized as experts. But so were other groups: biologists, medical doctors, and others—some with eugenicist views, others Malthusian ones—were also central in the ongoing discussions among professionals. But no one actor was recognized as having a position of authority, as superordinate relative to others who invested in and had an interest in what was at stake in this emerging field. All claimed to represent and speak on behalf of an imaginary constituency, advancing arguments about how society should be organized and governed in keeping with their positions, legitimized via claims to representation of the public good, all the while seeking to universalize their particularistic views by proclaiming their disinterestedness (see Bigo 2011, 247–48).

To account for how the OPR group became recognized as occupying a position of authority, we must analyze the specific positions and attendant forms and types of capital of the elite actors who were engaged in these debates. It is here that the OPR group's specific tailoring of knowledge production to those who had the resources to initiate action would prove important. Since the very early days of the MMF and later the OPR, members of this group had, more than their counterparts in other groups, specifically targeted and sought recognition primarily from such actors, not from their own academic peers.

Enter John D. Rockefeller III. Rockefeller had enormous wealth and was seeking to find his niche among the Rockefeller family's various philanthropic efforts. He also had political connections and could operate freely across various segments of American elite groups. He had funded a "survey trip" to Asia in 1948 because he was concerned that the Rockefeller Foundation's investments in public health efforts there were rendered futile by high population growth rates. He had also early on supported Sanger and the call for birth control in the US.

In preparing for the decision on how to proceed and what and how to fund population control efforts, Rockefeller organized a conference in Williamsburg, Virginia, in June 1952. The list of experts included the former US surgeon general, the president of MIT, and several past and future Nobel Prize laureates. Experts in botany, physics, embryology and economics as well as key figures in the Planned Parenthood Federation of America were invited. In addition, central demographic figures from the OPR—Notestein, Tauber, Davis, Whelpton, and Thompson—were present. The proceedings from the conference show first that while all in attendance shared an interest in the governance of population, there was a wide range of views as to how this should be done and why. Second, the OPR (Notestein in particular) enjoyed a position of some respectability compared to what some saw as "alarmists" and "radical" arguments.

For some conference participants, population growth was a problem related to the global scarcity of resources. Fairfield Osborn argued for identifying and working toward a global "optimum population." For Detlev Bronk, then president of the National Academy of Sciences and soon to become president of the Rockefeller Foundation, the central problem was "avoiding the potential degradation of the genetic quality of the human race" (quoted in Connelly 2008, 157). Heated debates revolved around whether "industrial development should be withheld from poor, agrarian countries like India" (157). Various solutions were discussed, including new energy sources and better technology for food production (McLean 1952b). Transition theory was therefore merely one among many different conceptions of population governance, and it was by no means given that those associated with the OPR would prevail and emerge with an element of authority vis-à-vis other actors who enjoyed no lower academic prestige.

Why, then, did Notestein and his colleagues come to prevail? Rockefeller's economic capital gave him a unique position from which to adjudicate among various proposals about how to proceed. In part because the Ford Foundation and other philanthropic efforts of the Rockefeller family were involved in other sectors—food production, energy, public health, development—Rockefeller was intent on finding a specific niche. He was already inclined to target fertility regulation—a topic still considered controversial—not least because he had already supported Sanger and the birth control movement at home for some time. More important, Notestein and his fellow demographers had been selected by Rockefeller to chair and guide important elements of the discussions at the Williamsburg conference.

Notestein in particular had a prominent position because he had several credentials also outside academia: not only had he formulated (with Tauber, Davis, and others) the framework of transition theory, he had subsequently served as director of the Population Division of the UN Secretariat (1946–48) and thus had accumulated a level of diplomatic experience. Notestein was consulted by Rockefeller's aide, John McLean, about whom to invite—but so were others, including Thomas Parran Jr., former surgeon general of the US Public Health Service, and Lewis Strauss of the Rockefeller Brothers Fund.[4] But after the conference, Rockefeller instructed his aide to "obtain from Notestein individually any ideas that he might have that developed at the conference as to the areas of opportunity of particular significance" (McLean 1952a).

It was Rockefeller's attention and solicitation of advice that anointed Notestein (with his colleagues) as primus inter pares among the actors who advanced slightly different conceptions of population governance: the primacy of economic capital from Rockefeller is central, but so are the extraacademic credentials associated with Notestein. That is, the actor with economic resources proved decisive because all of these actors were seeking recognition from those who would be able to fund and thus establish governance efforts, as all those who took part in these debates were first and foremost oriented toward action, not science.

Based on the advice from the Williamsburg conference, Rockefeller decided to set up a new organization, the Population Council. At its first board meeting in April 1953, the Population Council identified its focus in way that reflected the contents and implications of transition theory. It was decided that the organization would conduct work on three issues: the improvement and development of contraceptives, field testing of contraceptive methods, and studies in the psychology of acceptance in various geographical areas. The goal was to look "toward the practical application of knowledge for the control of the size and quality of human population in relation to total physical and cultural resources available in various areas and in the world as a whole" (Population Council 1953). When the Council started its operations in September 1953, it was established with two divisions that reflected this focus: a Demographic Division, and a Medical Division. The former was to conduct research on microlevel motivational and attitudinal aspects of fertility behavior, and on the macrolevel relation between national population growth rates and economic development; the latter would develop and test new contraceptives to be used in family planning programs.

The combination of economic and cultural or scientific capital—epitomized by the alliance between Notestein and Rockefeller—effectively settled the parameters of the emerging field and established transition theory anno 1949/1950 as the symbolic capital of the field. This did not happen through some magic trick of an omnipotent discourse, however. Rather, armed with economic resources, the framework of transition theory was given facticity inasmuch as new research programs were initiated at the Population Council to develop and test contraceptive methods, soon followed by family planning programs that delivered these contraceptives to developing countries. In short, a focus on means prevailed over a focus on motives, and the economic rationale for fertility regulation all but obliterated the health rationale.

Not only did this establish distinct boundaries between population and health as fields of governance, but it also demoted health professionals to a marginal position within the field of population. Transition theory—or more specifically the policy implications that flowed from it—became the field's symbolic capital to which all actors had to refer in their effort to receive recognition for their distinctive views. This had significant implications. For one thing, although family planning programs were staffed by health professionals, these programs were set up in order to achieve objectives—population control in the name of economic growth—that had little to do with health concerns. As these governing practices became established and institutionalized, actors who had different conceptions of governance anchored, say, in health concerns had no choice but to engage in debates about population governance on the terms set by the field's symbolic capital: health professionals were compelled to seek recognition on terms set by others, thus conferring authority—via the field's evaluative criterion—on superordinate actors. With a theoretical formulation as a blueprint for action, the field became structured in a way that reflected the distinctions and categories contained in transition theory: the dominant classification of this slice of social reality, itself the outcome of previous competition for authority, now became reflected in concrete practices, thereby giving it status as "second nature" and thus misrecognized as given and as structuring all actors' subsequent strategies.

Transnational, Not International: The Diffusion of the Field

In contrast to what we saw in chapters 2 and 3, the field of population was decidedly transnational rather than international. The terms of reference for the UN Population Commission, for example, were explicitly formulated to concern technical aspects and to maintain a "neutral" stance on whether population growth constituted a positive or negative force in relation to economic and social development. And while some governments, like those of India and Pakistan, had been pressing for UN involvement in advising on antinatalist policies, most newly independent states advanced a pronatalist stance. Catholic countries, whatever their stance on population growth as such, fiercely opposed any talk of contraception. The French delegate, drawing on a long history of French pronatalist policy, dismissed "le malthusianisme anglo-saxon," pointing to the lack of any internationally shared conceptualization of the dynamics and wider significance of population growth (Symonds and Carder 1973, 74). And given the controversies surrounding population policy within international organizations and at the domestic level in the US and elsewhere, there was no support for the establishment of a formal international policy to curb population growth.

The transnational trajectory of the field is important for an appreciation of the relatively marginal position of state actors. Rockefeller, as we have seen, was important precisely because no elected US official found it opportune to publicly support population control. Both Presidents Eisenhower and Kennedy privately supported population control abroad, but fears of alienating important domestic constituencies over contraceptive use and abortion meant that no official support or funding was forthcoming until the mid-1960s, by which time the field had already become transnationally organized and settled. Support from other Western donors, such as the UK and the Scandinavian countries, mattered, but these contributions were nowhere near the scale of funding available from the Rockefeller and Ford Foundation.

The diffusion and internationalization of fertility regulations in the name of economic growth was principally driven by the establishment of an transnational cadre of population professionals who developed careers within a range of nonstate organizations. When Western governments eventually came to support population control efforts, the modalities and cadre of specialists required to run governance efforts were already in place. Economic capital, then, had particular significance because of the lack of political capital: economic capital could be used to bypass political sanctioning and support via already established professional networks of family planning associations—as in India and Pakistan—who saw themselves as local intermediaries with Western counterparts in an effort to modernize their countries.

When the government of India decided to establish population control policies in late 1952, there was little funding available in the state budget.

This gave ample room for the Population Council, armed with technical expertise and money, to fund and shape the organization of population control efforts in India, which had been seen as the key area in which to launch population control since Sanger's days. The Population Council funded and designed training courses and helped set up research institutions devoted to population control in numerous developing countries, building an international cadre of experts steeped in transition theory and its attendant concept of governance—single-purpose family planning programs aimed at fertility regulation.

Starting in 1953, the Population Council established a fellowship program for the study of demography and related topics at US universities. By 1958, 69 fellowships had been awarded to individuals from 21 countries. In the course of the 1950s, nearly half of these fellows attended Notestein's OPR course on the demographic transition (Caldwell and Caldwell 1986, 12). As of 1961, 140 fellowships had been granted (Notestein 1961), and by 1968 the Population Council had awarded no fewer than 529 fellowships, 404 of these to individuals from the developing world (Notestein 1968, 554). At the institutional level, the Population Council was involved in establishing and funding the UN's regional demographic research and training centers in Bombay (1957), Santiago (1958), and Cairo (1963) (Critchlow 1999, 25). Moreover, the Council was involved in establishing or funding specialized research programs in family planning and related fields at the University of Chicago, Columbia University, the University of Michigan, the University of Pennsylvania, Boston University, Princeton University, Cornell University, the University of Minnesota, and Dartmouth College (Critchlow 1999, 240).

Writing in 1961, Notestein, then president of the Population Council, informed an official at the Rockefeller Brothers Fund that the Population Council was now the "principal source of technical assistance" in the field of population policy internationally (Critchlow 1999, 240). The governments of both India and Pakistan—the first in the developing world to establish family planning programs—had already requested assistance from the Population Council in formulating and organizing their population policies. In 1955, Notestein and Leona Baumgartner traveled to India to provide technical assistance. In 1959, the Population Council and the Ford Foundation supplied similar assistance to Pakistan. Caldwell and Caldwell (1986) note how the establishment of national population policy in Ghana "depended at every stage on committees, reports and calculations made by persons associated as faculty, students or both with the demography program at the University of Ghana, which had links with the London School of Economics and which was funded by the Population Council" (141–42). The Population Council also served as a key adviser to the governments of Taiwan, South Korea, Turkey, Tunisia, Thailand, Kenya, and Pakistan when these established national population policies in the 1960s (43).

In 1963, the Population Council established its Technical Assistance Division in response to the high demand from developing countries for expertise and know-how in establishing and organizing family planning programs (Rockefeller Archive Center 1963). Many of the research centers established at various universities now began to provide technical assistance to developing countries: the population research centers at Michigan, Harvard, Johns Hopkins, North Carolina, Chicago, and Pittsburgh were all directly involved in providing technical assistance, giving courses, and sending personnel to help establish population programs in the developing world (Rockefeller Archive Center 1965, 1).

The diffusion of the new practice of family planning did not operate through normative suasion, learning, or "internalization," as is implied in the literature on advocacy networks and epistemic communities (cf. Risse 2012). Rather, it thrived on elite-to-elite exchange of valuable symbolic and material resources within an emerging transnational field (Dezalay and Garth 2002): Sanger and other birth controllers had helped establish a global network of national family planning associations that had been pushing for population control long before other Western experts offered to fund or help design such policies. These associations were typically headed by elites with either cultural capital (professional credentials such as medical degrees) or social capital (close links to high-ranking public officials). The director of the Family Planning Association of India, Dhanvanthi Rama Rau, an ally of Sanger's, was married to the governor of the Bank of India and was instrumental in getting population control into India's first Five-Year Plan in 1952. Similarly, the director of Pakistan's family planning association was married to the country's foreign minister and was similarly central in getting the government to support family planning clinics in 1957 (Connelly 2008, 184–85). In India, proponents of family planning were part of a Western-educated middle class that "drew upon the intellectual capital available from the West" and "redeployed it for specific political projects such as bourgeois nationalism and family reforms within the context of colonial India" (Ahluwalia 2007, 25). As historian Matthew Connelly (2008, 285) explains, the family planning effort "began in most countries by organizing local elites into an association, typically including expatriates and dominated by doctors, which then sought out a prominent politician or his wife as a patron." India was a prime location where Western proponents of population control "contended to accumulate cultural and economic capital, prestige and patronage, as well as markets for their newly developed contraceptive technologies" (Ahluwalia 2007, 55). These elite contacts were matched with a significant investment in training of personnel to staff and head family planning programs in developing countries. With family planning programs rapidly established in the developing world during the 1960s, a sizable investment was made, primarily in the United States, to set up specialized training programs and university courses within schools of public health to educate family planning administrators who would either work in or provide advice to developing countries. Starting in 1963, the Ford Foundation made concerted efforts to institutionalize such programs and courses so that graduates could advise, run, and staff family planning programs. The collaboration among the Ford Foundation and Johns Hopkins University, Princeton University, the University of Pennsylvania, the University of Chicago, the University of North Carolina, the University of Michigan, and Harvard University demonstrates this dynamics of how conceptualizing fertility behavior as an object of government in this particular way resulted in the buildup of a new type of expertise in family planning administration. Reminiscing about his time as key population officer at the Ford Foundation, Oscar Harkavy (1995) noted that the university research and training centers were central in institutionalizing family planning:

> Some thousand graduate students from the United States and the Third World took degrees from these centers. . . . Graduates of these centers found themselves in key positions in the population movement as researchers, teachers and program administrators. (86)

This trajectory is important, for its vehicle and speed were based on its transnational character: in 1965, globally available funds for efforts to reduce population growth came primarily from the Ford Foundation ($10.7 million), the Population Council ($2.3 million), the Rockefeller Foundation ($3.2 million), the US Agency for International Development ($2.3 million), and the International Planned Parenthood Federation ($0.9 million). Not until 1968 did a governmental source, the US Agency for International Development, surpass the nongovernmental sources of funding.

Therefore, when international organizations became involved—when the UN established its Trust Fund for Population Activities (later the UN Population Fund) in 1969 and when UNESCO, UNICEF, the Food and Agriculture Organization, and WHO became involved in providing funds and technical assistance—the contents, hierarchies, and boundaries of the field of population had already been thoroughly institutionalized at the transnational level and taken on a status as second nature, misrecognized as given and universally valid by virtue of the categories through which governance practices were designed and managed. It is a testament to how a field determines the relative efficacy of material and symbolic resources that leading figures in this field had enough clout to convince the UN secretary-general that the UN Population Fund should operate without oversight from member states but instead be guided by a handpicked council of advocates of population control policies. Only when specific intergovernmental venues were set up to receive governmental support did claims about speaking on behalf of a particular government matter and then only temporarily.

Field Boundaries and the Hierarchy of Professional Groups: Motives versus Means, Health versus Economics

Transition theory came to constitute the field's symbolic capital, and I detail its effects on the social topography and boundaries of the field through a discussion of the marginal position of health workers and of the boundary between population and health as distinct fields. Transition defined fertility regulation and population control as instruments of economic policy, with scant focus on health aspects. This sheds light not only on the boundaries and tensions between health and population as distinct fields but also on the hierarchy between demographers and health professionals within the field of population itself. The subordination of health professionals was produced in no small part by the building of a cadre of health professionals who specialized and made careers within the field of population. At a 1964 conference in New York organized by the Population Council on Strategy for Implementing Family Planning in Developing Countries, a revealing discussion unfolded about the need for training personnel to run and staff family planning programs. It was pointed out that while there were certain inadequacies in these training programs within the schools of public health, "public health is the professional identity of family planning workers in these countries." Therefore, "we have little choice but to encourage US schools of public health to do their best" (Rockefeller Archive Center 1964, 8–9). Dudley Kirk brings out with great clarity how the field's evaluative criterion defined the context within which the role of medical and health personnel was determined. In a 1964 memo to Notestein, Kirk commented on the "Role of Private Medical Profession and Health Occupations":

Historically, family planning has progressed largely in *spite of* the medical profession, but with the IUD the basic situation may well have changed; the medical and para-medical professions will play a key role and can have a great weight either positively or negatively. There is a need for great involvement not only for the services they can perform but to give family planning "respectability." (3; emphasis added)

The training of health professionals to run family planning programs was informed by another rationale as well: health considerations could serve as a legitimizing and motivating factor in efforts to persuade people to regulate their fertility. In discussing the challenges related to family planning as a means to reduce fertility rates, Berelson (1969), for example, explained why family planning is the "first step taken on the road to population control":

because from a broad political standpoint it is the most acceptable one: *since it is closely tied to maternal and child health care it can be perceived as a health measure beyond dispute*; and since voluntary it can be justified as a contribution to the effective personal freedom of individual couples. On both scores, the practice ties into accepted values and thus achieves political viability. (1)

In one commentator's summary, the field was so configured that:

economic and social policies were determined primarily by economists and planners located in ministries or special agencies in close contact with the leaders of government. Population policies and programmes originated with this group. But they were carried out largely by men who occupied subordinate positions in a health ministry which generally lacked influence in the hierarchy of government offices. (Whitney 1976, 341)

Writing in 1976, Finkle and Crane reflected on this tension within the field of population as they explored the role of the World Health Organization (WHO) in population policy:

The controversy begins with the question of whether birth control information and services should be delivered in conjunction with health services or separately from them. WHO officials and most health administrators hold the position that regardless of the demographic aims of family planning programs, these programs should be integrated as closely as possible with health services. Others, including many population specialists, take the view that fertility limitation is too urgent a task to leave to health organizations and that there are alternative, more effective ways of implementing programs to reduce fertility that require little, if any, involvement of health services and medical personnel. (368)

For health professionals and the WHO in particular, it was imperative that funds should not be diverted from health services to family planning. As M. G. Candau, director-general of the WHO, declared at the nineteenth World Health Assembly in 1966, "Countries are deviating funds from public health in order to carry out family planning. . . . I think we should continue to fight in the World Health Organization for improvement of health services and not for deviation of funds to other types of services" (Candau 1966, 2). Yet one decade later, even the World Health Assembly, dominated by health professionals, concluded that while health concerns should always remain primary, the WHO could "give technical advice, upon request, in the development of activities in family planning, *as part of an organized health service, without impairing its normal preventive and curative functions*" (Finkle and Crane 1976, 375). Public health professionals and obstetricians and gynecologists were involved in running family planning programs in the developing world, but their position had become marginal due to the evaluation criterion against which they sought recognition as actors in the field of population. Health experts continually sought to invoke arguments grounded in a commitment to health and to challenge the primacy of economic considerations in family planning programs, but during the period when the field was becoming institutionalized at the global level, these arguments were marginalized. To take one example, WHO efforts to channel investments in population control efforts into broader health issues were unsuccessful, despite the organization's authority in matters relating to health.

Conclusion

Armed with considerable economic resources, a relatively small group of actors managed to build a transnational field whose boundaries and internal hierarchies can be traced back to a set of fundamental distinctions that flowed from how the theory of demographic transition had been initially formulated and reformulated in the attempt to secure recognition from those who could initiate governance efforts. Occupying marginal positions in university circles, the demographers associated with the Milbank Memorial Fund and the Office of Population Research not only targeted actors with the resources to initiate action programs but reformulated and fine-tuned their argumentation so it could guide governance efforts. Having been anointed as authoritative figures through the financial support of John D. Rockefeller III and the establishment of the Population Council, these actors constructed a field that was marked by a supply-side approach; the focus was on delivering the means to regulate fertility rather than seeking to influence people's motives for doing so. And health matters became subordinate to—and chiefly a legitimizing factor of—practices aimed at achieving economic objectives. Because of the genesis of the field, established and institutionalized through investments in research and training, the ongoing competition over positions of authority played out at the level of knowledge production.

On the one hand, we need to account for the initial establishment of authority with reference to competition for recognition among a myriad of actors, all seeking to advance their preferred conception of governance. But in analyzing the gradual evolution of this field, we must also understand the terms on which authority could be recognized. Actors not only compete for positions of authority by accumulating resources and bringing these to bear within a given field. They also seek to change the evaluative criteria within any given field. As we shall see in the next chapter, the distinctions between means and motives, between health and economics, were central to the stakes of the field. An epistemic communities approach can account for the existence of a group of demographers whose ideas policymakers adopted because they were uncertain about what to do. And an account with basis in transnational advocacy network can similarly reference the network of actors mobilized around an agenda defined by actors with a level of moral authority.

However, such an account would ignore crucial facts: that there was ongoing competition between distinct actors; that population control emerged transnationally outside (at least initially) intergovernmental support; that the mechanism of diffusion depended on building up a cadre of population specialists and elite contacts in developing countries and not on socialization or internalization; and finally that the very contents of transition theory (and by implication the boundaries and internal structure of the field) were themselves outcomes of past struggles over how to classify and act on the world, driven by a search for recognition on the part of actors who had the resources to put population theories into action. More fundamentally, the actors involved here can be said to have been an epistemic community, a transnational advocacy network, a profession, and a transnational governance network directly engaged in governing. But as we have seen, such categorizations of actor attributes fail to capture the extent to which the nature of these actors changed over time, individually and as a larger group according to the genesis of the field, the practices they engaged in, and the changing character of their relations with each other and their environment (cf. McAdam, Tarrow, and Tilly 2002).

CHAPTER 5

Safeguarding Positions, Transforming the Field

The Field Population of 1974–1994

In 1994, at the UN-organized International Conference on Population and Development in Cairo, state representatives met to negotiate a new international population policy. The outcome document—the "Cairo consensus"—was seen as remarkable in that it did not contain a single reference to "population growth" as a problem. The new "consensus" was organized around the concept of "reproductive health and rights" that had been advocated by a transnational advocacy network of women's groups and health professionals. These actors had challenged the primacy of macrolevel concerns with population growth as a cause of underdevelopment and formulated a policy focused on the health needs and human rights of women. This they had done by producing and mobilizing new knowledge around the concept of maternal and child health, by establishing venues for transnational mobilization between women's groups in the Global South and the North, and by allying with organizations such as the World Health Organization (WHO).

As such, this is a story that would seem to fit well with the literature on transnational advocacy networks or on epistemic communities, depending on whether the emphasis is on "moral" or "epistemic" authority: a group of actors forge a set of norms or knowledge claims and attendant policy prescriptions that they succeed in getting on the agenda and eventually adopt as policy through such key causal mechanisms as mobilization, shaming, persuasion, or some form of socialization. But the analytical categories thereby imposed, organized around a set of actor attributes and their ideal-typical strategies, cannot capture the centrality of the field-specific positions from which this advocacy or policy influence was performed. Without an account of the changes in what could be construed as a "source" of authority, moreover, it is difficult to explain the dynamics, timing, and effects of the changes that did take place in this field.

In fact, the transformation that occurred with the Cairo conference—hailed by its proponents and by commentators as the success of transnational advocacy efforts—was in many respects not a transformation. Rather, dominant actors in the field, forced to defend their position against a broad array of heterodox arguments, reengineered the field's criterion of evaluation (its symbolic capital) so as to perpetuate their own positions, now under a new heading. The changes that we can observe from the new consensus developed at the Cairo conference are better explained in terms of competition within the field over positions of authority and over what should count as relevant and significant claims about population governance. The symbolic divisions that structured the field served to accord some actors a position from which they could recognize, disregard, or ridicule claims made about population governance depending on whether these corresponded to the field's evaluative criterion.

The 1994 Cairo conference as well as the 1974 Bucharest conference and the 1984 Mexico City conference were important not because of their formal position as intergovernmental conferences dominated by states but because they reduced the relative autonomy of the field by allowing actors to bring capital accruing from the outside to bear on the field.

The analysis is organized around the *nomos*—the "principle of vision and division" (Bourdieu 1999, 68)—of the field as analyzed in chapter 4 in terms of the distinctions between means and motives and between economics and health. These two distinctions were important for establishing the field of population as something distinct from development and from health. Changes in the field's relative autonomy over time came to increase the value of the positions marked by credentials from both of these fields. I thus bring out the extent to which transnational fields are not fully autonomous (Gorski 2013; Vauchez 2011), which makes them susceptible to changes as an effect of changes in the "spaces between" fields (Eyal 2013). The Population Council figures prominently in the analysis, not only because of its central position in the field but also because it can serve as a prism for studying the dominant actors in the field as compared to those occupying subordinate positions who sought to undermine the field's hierarchies.

The *Nomos* and Configuration of the Field

Transition theory constituted the field's evaluative criterion in terms of how the categories through which actors understood and acted in the world were products of that theory. This also extended to the production of knowledge: The whole subdiscipline of population studies emerged as part and parcel of the efforts aimed at using knowledge production and the training of specialists as a means of exporting population control efforts to developing countries. As Susan Greenhalgh (2012) has argued, "population studies" was no academic subdiscipline but an "opportunistic assemblage" of methods and political concerns whose orientation and concerns were structured by the concerns of practitioners (121). Moreover, this particular assemblage of research techniques, put to use for a highly specific purpose, was created by researchers from the very same organizations that were involved in designing and running family planning programs. The Population Council's research on fertility regulation coexisted within the same organization as the funding and management of practices aimed at such regulation in the form of family planning programs (Hodgson 1988, 563). It was this fusion of tasks at the Population Council, at the International Planned Parenthood Federation (IPPF), and at the Guttmacher Institute and as well as various US universities that became involved in "action programs" that made the evaluative criterion strong and the field "settled" in Steinmetz's (2008a) sense—that is, with all actors, including subordinate ones, recognizing and valuing the same principle of hierarchization.

Professors in, say, demography or sociology were unable to translate their academic credentials if they did not have ties to and were deemed relevant by the key actors in the field—i.e., those engaged in governance efforts. This was produced by the particular genesis of this field, where organizations such as the Population Council had vast resources to invest in social scientific and medical research as well as extensive training of professionals and the direct management of family planning programs. Positions at otherwise prestigious universities thereby became subordinated to those within or tied to such organizations. A distinct hybrid discipline, population studies, emerged and, in the words of Dennis Hodgson (1988) "acquired all the characteristics of a well-institutionalized intellectual activity" (563)—but one that had a highly specific focus, aimed at increasing the efficacy of a preset objective: to curb population growth. The field was characterized by competition for authority on scientific terms, but the actors in a position to accord or withhold recognition were principally "managers" of population control programs rather than professors at university departments.

Competing for Authority I: Means versus Motives

Efforts to reduce population growth in the developing world assumed the form of family planning programs aimed at supplying means to regulate fertility rather than seeking to change the motivation or conditions under which such means were used. This was partly a response to the felt urgency of the need to reduce population growth as a tool in the ideological competition with communism but also a reference to the classical Malthusian argument about the world's "carrying capacity" and the prospects of a "population bomb" (Raulet 1970, 213). This served as the background for efforts to change fertility behavior that did not address its structural causes, as that approach was deemed too slow, too complex, and too costly. Moreover, family planning programs—purportedly based on the "voluntary choice" and "consent of individuals"—had since long found support in national-level birth control movements in the West and in certain developing countries. For example, information about family planning services was introduced in the final text from the UN Human Rights Conference in Tehran in 1968 and was further specified to include family planning services in a UN General Assembly resolution the following year.[1]

The distinction between a focus on means and a focus on motivational aspects flowed from the tension within transition theory, as detailed in chapter 4, with means (or a supply-side approach) gaining the upper hand. This had significant implications for the relative autonomy of a separate field of population, for it meant that the very autonomy or rationale for a separate field of population governance was threatened by claims that investments in development, and thus motivational change, would be most effective in reducing population growth (and thereby spurring economic development).

From the very start, recognition of the significance of motivational change was an integral albeit subordinated part of the evolution of the field in terms of what was at stake. To grasp how the field came to evolve, we need to understand what claims were made, from which positions, and with what effects on the direction of the policy debate.

The most important resource for those in dominant positions to fend off criticism was the wealth of ostensibly objective data produced through the "Knowledge, Attitude, Practice" (KAP) studies. The Population Council, for example, received a total of $75 million from the US Agency for International Development (USAID) for operations research on family planning programs in the developing world (Harkavy 1995, 83). KAP studies measure the "KAP gap," or what was interpreted as an "unmet need" for family planning services. They were the most significant form of knowledge production within the newly formed subdiscipline of "family planning research," which had been established with the explicit rationale of improving the efficacy of family planning programs and helping persuade political leaders in the developing world of their significance.

The KAP studies were explicitly aimed at analyzing "motives" but in a way tailored to identify the "market" or "unmet need" for family planning rather than measuring or adjudicating between supply-side and demand-side approaches. As such, they were central in the perpetuating the field's evaluative criterion by objectifying a definition and measure of "motives" that served to underwrite a supply-side approach. Reviewing the relevance of KAP-type surveys, Stycos noted in 1964, "The most important function of such surveys is similar to any market research project: to demonstrate the existence of a demand for goods or services, in this case for birth control" (368). He went on to stress the immediate political significance, echoing the idea of introducing controversial policies under the aegis of scientific knowledge: "A third function of such studies relates to the fact that research is a relatively uncontroversial way of initiating activity in population control, in countries where direct efforts are not possible" (368).

As the standard-bearers of what constituted proper research, KAP studies and the measurement of "unmet need" perpetuated the field's evaluative criterion by taking up a concern with motivational aspects of fertility—which potentially pointed beyond the field of population proper to the field of development interventions (poverty reduction, education, and so forth)—and transforming it into a relevant aspect that could improve the acceptance, efficacy, and spread of family planning programs.[2]

The extent to which the political commitment to population control came to shape policy debates and funding priorities of research on population change is aptly captured by Demeny's (1988) observation that "social science provided the rationale for the creation of the population industry but, once established, the industry took command" (463). Another commentator described the new field of "family planning studies" as

> the systematic study of the phenomenon of family planning among populations, of the processes by which the practice of family planning diffuses through a community or nation, and of the forces that retard or facilitate such diffusion or adoption. (Bogue 1966, 721)

The subfield of family planning was institutionalized as an integral part of the key organizations in the field. In 1964 came *Studies in Family Planning*, published by the Population Council, and *Family Planning Perspectives*, published by the Alan Guttmacher Institute. In 1975, the latter established *International Family Planning Perspectives*.[3] The period between 1962 and 1968, when family planning programs were established in the developing world at an increasing pace, saw a qualitative shift in the content of such publications toward a "markedly higher development in field experiments, studies of incentives and evaluative-type researches" (Hill 1968, 985). In both periods covered in Hill's study (1955–61 and 1962–68), KAP studies rank highest of the total output of publications, at 21.1 percent and 21.9 percent, respectively.

It is a testament to the particular configuration and stakes of this field that an individual with impeccable academic credentials in demography, Kingsley Davis—one of the original formulators of transition theory, together with Frank Notestein and Irene Tauber at the Princeton's Office for Population Research—was debunked with reference to data from KAP surveys when he challenged the hierarchy between means and motives. Writing in the prestigious *Science* magazine, from his position as professor of sociology at the University of California at Berkeley, Davis sought to make his academic credentials to have purchase on debates in the field. Davis (1967) argued that proponents of family planning proponents were

> forever talking about "attitudes" and "needs." But they pose the issue
> in terms of the "acceptance" of birth control devices. At the most
> naïve level, they assume that lack of acceptance is a function of the
> contraceptive device itself. *This reduces the motive problem to a techno-*
> *logical question.* (733)

He went on to say that by understanding "negative attitudes towards birth control as due to ignorance, apathy and outworn tradition, and 'mass communication' as the solution to the motivation problem, family planners tend to *ignore the power and complexity of social life*" (733). Davis's main point was that it was essential to move "beyond family planning" and focus on altering those "systems of rewards and punishments" that determine the character of fertility behavior within any specific cultural and socioeconomic setting—a focus on motivational change, in other words.

However, the dominant institutions in the field—the Population Council, the Ford Foundation, Planned Parenthood, and others—viewed him as an outsider, with no connections to or influence on those in positions to decide on the design and management of family planning programs. In a rare move, indicating that one had to explicitly defend orthodoxy rather than simply operating on the basis of doxic acceptance, Bernard Berelson (1969), president of the Population Council, defended the commitment to family planning programs against this criticism: he declared, "We are undertaking a virtually unprecedented effort at deliberate social change of a very great magnitude" and listed a wide range of difficulties that characterized family planning programs (1). He sought to defend the efficacy and viability of family planning programs by referring to an Organisation for Economic Co-Operation and Development (OECD) analysis that had found that 2.3 million births had been averted in 1968. Whereas that study had in fact concluded on this basis that family planning programs had limited success, Berelson (1969) argued that this "impact could reasonably be interpreted as substantial indeed" (6).[4]

Kingsley Davis was not alone in noting that an effective response to the population problem would require moving "beyond" family planning. There came a steady stream of statements indicating that the gravity of the problem and the character of fertility behavior necessitated efforts targeting the demand side of the equation. Paul Ehrlich's widely read *The Population Bomb*, published in 1968, contained numerous references to the need to impose nonvoluntary measures of fertility control, such as placing temporary sterilization agents in water supplies and food staples. Garrett Hardin's frequently cited "The Tragedy of the Commons" (1968) similarly referred to "mutual coercion" as a possible response to population growth. Kenneth Boulding (1964) even suggested the creation of a system under which licenses to have children could be distributed and sold, while Sripati Chandresekhar mentioned compulsory sterilization as well as the possibility that "every married couple in India deny themselves sexual intercourse for a year" (Berelson 1969, 13). But these authors' academic credentials had little purchase on the evaluative criterion that had been established in the field, which, although based on the production of knowledge, was specifically aimed at making family planning programs more efficient: being forced to seek recognition in terms of categories now firmly institutionalized and linked to action programs, these interventions were of little significance.

The 1960s and early 1970s saw significant political changes in the US, with the civil rights movement and the war in Vietnam as central factors. Some now saw population control as a thinly veiled imperialist project (Mamdani 1972); others, among them Linda Gordon (1974), identified the strong links between the eugenics concerns prevalent among US elites and family planning programs (as discussed in chapter 3). Such criticism, however, did not gain much traction, owing in no small part to the force of the categories through which those in the field defined their object of governance. As Hodgson (1988) observed, "Such questioning of scientific legitimacy by 'unmasking' ideological roots was usually ignored by orthodox demographers" (556).

Already by the late 1960s there had emerged criticism from within the discipline of economics concerning the economic rationale for population control. Both Kuznets (1967) and Easterlin (1967) forcefully argued that claims about a strong causal relation between population growth and economic growth were unfounded. This attack against the economic rationale for population control was excluded from serious consideration and debate within population studies. Whenever the precise economic dynamics at work were under debate, such attacks were dismissed as "academic" or "theoretical," as failing to reflect how family planning helped provide services in demand in developing countries. Julian Simon, a leading figure among those economists who contested the claim that investment in population control yielded high returns in terms of growth, is a case in point. His *The Economics of Population Growth* (1977) and *The Ultimate Resource* (1981) challenged the very rationale for a separate policy field of population. Oscar Harkavy (1995), head of the Ford Foundation's population program at the time, noted later that

> whenever we encountered one another at professional meetings, Simon would chide me for not supporting his work. When I protested that he never asked, he said: "What's the use. You never would have funded me anyway." I must admit he probably was right because those from whom I took advice were not impressed by Simon's writings. (83)

Both Simon and Davis sought to convert their forms of capital (academic credentials in economics and demography) in an effort to make a mark on the debate by attacking either the privileging of means over motives (Davis) or the presumed causal link between population control and economic growth (Simon) (Cf. Hodgson 1988, 556). Reflecting on her own first experience with these debates in the early 1970s, Joan Dunlop makes clear the extent to which the field was autonomous, operating in a microcosmos whose categories and principles of distinction shielded it from broader developments in its environment. Dunlop, then working as assistant to John D. Rockefeller III, reflects on her first meetings as a member of the Population Council's board:

I would listen to these conversations about contraception and it was very hard not to feel repulsed because women were being treated as objects and a means to an end. . . . And then I became increasingly puzzled by this, because I had come out of, not the civil rights movement exactly, but I had worked for some extraordinary people in the Ford Foundation [on domestic issues]. And I had learned a lot about racism, my own and what it was and how to read it. And I felt the racism in this field. I just could—it was palpable. And also, I thought that it was also terribly innocent, in a curious way. People did not understand what they were saying or what their values implied. . . . I don't know what's going on here. It's as though people who did international work have lived in a different planet and that the civil rights movement of the last ten years or fifteen years in the United States never touched them. They lived elsewhere, outside of the Earth. (2004, 5–6)

The field had established categories and classifications—now firmly institutionalized—that constructed a world with distinct hierarchies and positions almost impenetrable to outside criticism. This interlocking between knowledge-production and governance efforts had profound effects on who mattered. In 1972, for example, Berelson concluded in an internal memo to his colleagues at the Population Council that there was mounting opposition from developing countries against family planning programs (see Critchlow 1999, 177–78). A conference organized by the International Planned Parenthood Federation in England had confirmed concerns about a "backlash," whereas Robert McNamara, as president of the World Bank, had learned that many developing countries had begun to see family planning as "too simple, too narrow, and too coercive" (Critchlow 1999, 178). But such criticisms from actors claiming to represent those subject to family planning programs in the developing world were not seen as a significant part of the debates in the field itself. Even though criticism against population policy was registered by the early 1970s, organizations like the Population Council began preparations for the 1974 UN World Population Conference in Bucharest with the expectation that now, for the first time, there would come intergovernmental approval for more ambitious targets in controlling population growth.

However, the Bucharest conference brought a split between governments from the developing world and Western governments precisely over whether "population" could and should be seen as separate from efforts aimed at improving people's economic welfare and thus as distinct from the field of development.

Loss of Autonomy: Bucharest Backlash

Any field can be said to be "autonomous" if external events are mediated by the field itself and have little direct bearing on its dynamics (Steinmetz 2008a, 596; cf. Cohen 2011). Fields of a transnational character are, in this reading, relatively autonomous to the extent that they function according to laws that cannot be reduced to structuring events in their environment. In this context, intergovernmental forums like the Bucharest conference and later those in Mexico City and in Cairo constituted "interventions" in the functioning of the field, making it subject to claims made by actors whose resources came from outside the field as such. With these conferences came a new dynamic that reduced (temporarily) the strength of the evaluative criteria of the field: Developing countries converted the capital accruing from representing a territorially delimited constituency to challenge the strict boundary between "population" and "development."

Western governments came to Bucharest advocating population control through family planning programs. The US delegation, headed by Caspar Weinberger, called for an inclusion in the Plan of Action that population growth rates at the national level were to be set to a target of 1.2 percent. Most developing countries countered with an argument that threatened to undermine the very unity of and rationale for a separate policy field of "population" as defined by its reliance on family planning programs. Successful curbing of population growth, they held, would require large-scale investment in economic development to alter the socioeconomic and cultural conditions that fostered high fertility rates. This position was epitomized by the words of India's minister of health, Dr. Karan Singh: "Development is the best contraceptive." (quoted in Sinding 2000, 1842)[5] This statement summarized the implications not only of a demand-side approach to population control but also to the thinking behind the new international economic order.

Criticisms from developing countries were important to the degree that they blocked any hopes of agreeing—at an intergovernmental level—on specific targets for population control at the Bucharest conference. As a transnational field dominated by actors with access to economic resources and elite connections in target states, this did not necessarily constitute a problem. The conference was important insofar as it reduced the autonomy of the field and thus allowed criticism to be voiced and recognized by other states. But there was little direct impact on established practice and hierarchies in the field.

What did matter was a statement by the individual who had served as midwife for the very creation of the field as such, John D. Rockefeller III. At a side event organized by NGOs, Rockefeller stunned his colleagues and friends with a speech in which he confessed, "I now strongly believe that the only viable course is to place population policy solidly within the context of general economic and social development" (1974, 4). Here, Rockefeller was effectively criticizing his colleagues and established policy for the dominant focus on the means aspect of fertility regulation and for not addressing the motivational aspect more comprehensively, through investment in development efforts. In substance echoing the criticism of population policy made by developing countries, Rockefeller took a position that invested the critique with authority. With his wealth and attendant connections in business and political circles, being in the field but not of it, Rockefeller occupied a unique position, able to operate in and shape other, adjacent areas of US philanthropy. The background for his unprecedented speech urging a rethink of the field of population, came from his involvement in similar activities in the US. In the early 1970s, Rockefeller had hired Dunlop, telling her, "Something is wrong with population. Spend a year and talk to people and find out" (Dunlop 2004).

Dunlop helped author Rockefeller's speech together with Adrienne Germain, whom Dunlop had hired on the advice of a former colleague at the Ford Foundation. Dunlop and Germain drew on criticisms of family planning programs from anthropologists and others who concluded that family planning programs had been inattentive to the concerns and rights of women and thus also inefficient. This pointed toward a "demand-side" approach, where "investments in employment, education, basic health, and a better distribution of income and social services" were recognized as important (Critchlow 1999, 179).[6] And it was this line of reasoning that found its way into Rockefeller's speech. Declaring that the family planning programs had "proved inadequate when compared to the magnitude of the problems facing us," Rockefeller said that antinatalist efforts should be integrated within general social and economic development and concluded that "new and urgent attention to the role of women was essential to any development program" (181).

Reactions from the Population Council were strong. Without directly confronting the chair of the board, the organization's 1974 Annual Report observed, for example, that intergovernmental meetings such as the Bucharest conference represented a problem. Once governments get involved in such debates, the report noted, the issue inevitably becomes "politicized." The "reasonable discourse" of demographers and population specialists was now in jeopardy, since the Bucharest conference had introduced "polemical arguments" where the "issue becomes a useful tool with which to pursue existing political disagreements" (20) The report, authored by Berelson, who had resigned in protest after the Bucharest conference, concluded, "To a large extent, the debate at Bucharest was dominated by a Third World definition of the 'problem' and a Third World designation of the 'solution.' Through it all, the demographic trends go on, and so does the work of this organization" (21, 24).

Despite the shake-up at the Bucharest conference, funds for population policy from all the major donors—the World Bank, the UN Population Fund (UNFPA), USAID, Norway, Sweden, and the United Kingdom—continued to go to family planning programs. Moreover, USAID, the IPPF, and the Pathfinder Fund all defined their role as being "educators," engaging in "consciousness-raising" through knowledge and informational campaigns regarding family planning programs targeted at policy elites and the public in the developing world. And the UNFPA—operating on the basis of a wide interpretation of its mandate—was involved in promoting family planning programs even in countries that had no population policy (Wolfson 1983, 12).

However, the changes at the Population Council in keeping with Rockefeller's new reasoning were to prove significant. After Berelson resigned following Rockefeller's speech, it took the Board of Trustees three years to identify a new candidate, not least because the entire rationale for the organization had now been put in question (Connelly 2008, 332–33). Pushed by Dunlop and Germain, Rockefeller opted for George Zeidenstein. In contrast to all previous presidents of the Council, Zeidenstein had a background in the field of development.

Competing for Authority II: Health versus Economics

The distinction between motives and means had structured the competition for authority by consistently subordinating the former to the latter, in no small part through investment in specific types of research, like the KAP studies. But the relative dearth of serious challenges to the established hierarchy also had to do with the weaker position of actors with a background in development work in terms of professional institutionalization and academic prestige. In this context, the subordination of health concerns in the field of population seems all the more puzzling. After all, medical doctors had societal prestige and a high degree of professionalization and were central in producing new contraceptive technology, both as staff in family planning programs and as managers of these programs. Efforts to render fertility behavior governable required a sizable mobilization of biomedical research, as well as midwives, gynecologists, and public health administrators to manage and staff family planning programs. Unsurprisingly, most national family planning programs that were established in the developing world became the operational responsibility of the national ministries of health. While the ultimate objectives of these programs were formulated by national planning boards that set economically motivated demographic targets, the actual programs were organized and run by personnel with a primary commitment to and focus on the health of the individual.

As we saw in chapter 4, the subordination of health to economics emerged with the conceptual aggregation of fertility behavior implied in transition theory: once national society replaced the family as the level of analysis, the mutually reinforcing relationship between economic welfare and health was broken. Health-based arguments advanced by actors with credentials in the field of health had purchase only to the degree that they were oriented toward and sought recognition from the field's criterion of evaluation. For example, Allan G. Rosenfield (1976), a prominent public health scholar, sought to transcend established tensions by using his health-specific capital to gain recognition as a relevant interlocutor in the field, arguing that

> although physicians, public health personnel, demographers and economists and sociologists have discussed at length the most appropriate ways to proceed at this point, debates on whether "within" or "beyond" family planning is the best approach are unnecessary. Rather, those involved in family planning and population programs should carefully consider ways to improve existing family planning programs. (115)

Similarly, the 1977 Annual Report of the Population Council, now under the leadership of Zeidenstein, explicitly linked the criticisms of the supply-side mode of intervention with a call to a focus on the "health needs of the individual and thus improve the efficacy of family planning programs" (22). The Population Council was thus no less committed to population control, and the health dimension of reproduction was invoked very much as a means to the end of increased efficacy. The report further noted, "Because childbearing imposes large health risks on mothers, and the health risks to newborn and young children are also high, contraceptive materials, services and information should be a required part of every primary health care system." But it went on to add: "This does not mean that health care systems should be the only, or even the main, channels for delivering contraception. Nor does it mean that contraception can be considered exclusively, or even primarily, a health service" (23–24).

In contrast, the director-general of WHO, Halfdan Mahler of Denmark (1979), accused population policy of "imposing a vertical structure which has nothing to do with people's understanding" (quoted in Crane 1993, 365), thus challenging the marginal position of the health rationale for fertility regulation but also mobilizing health professionals to contest their subordinate position in family planning programs. A significant body of literature emerged in the 1970s from within the field of health that addressed the relation between population dynamics and health in general and family planning and health in particular. It is a testament to the force of the field's pull, however, that, as Barbara Crane (1993) notes, most of the criticism "focused on the means by which population programs were being implemented, and on the need for higher quality of care and for mechanisms to assure voluntarism in the delivery of family planning services. [Critics'] stance was more reformist than oppositional" (365).

At the WHO, which had long aimed to wrestle the regulation of fertility out of the hands of population-control proponents, a Special Programme in Research, Development, and Research Training in Human Reproduction (HRP) was established as early as 1972 in an effort to become involved in and have say on the development, testing, and use of different contraceptives (Oudshoorn 1997). Over time, the HRP came to include in its portfolio a focus on the broader health aspects of fertility regulation and contraceptive methods. But even the WHO—preeminent among international health organizations—initially took a stance that clearly deferred to and sought recognition from those in positions of authority in the field of population. The 1978–79 WHO biennial report[7] introduced the discussion of the operations of the HRP by noting the existence of "hardware" enthusiasts emphasizing a supply-side mode of intervention, "software" enthusiasts emphasizing a demand-side mode of intervention to regulate fertility behavior, and a third group, the HRP, which "recognizes the shortcomings of both hardware and software, but also their interdependence" (WHO 1980, 69). The HRP is presented as a research program "concerned with both hardware and software" (Ibid.). However, the description of the activities of the HRP shows the extent to which the "software" dimension of fertility regulation had been addressed only cursorily compared to its research on "hardware" in terms of developing and testing contraceptive technology (Ibid., 75). The 1980–81 biennial report makes reference to a new project in two rural areas in Kenya, summarizing what was to become a centerpiece of the critique of family planning programs—"the introduction of the concept of planning their families without any attention being given to other aspects of their lives . . . had confirmed them in the opinion that family limitation was in the interest of 'other people' with ulterior motives, not in their own interests" (WHO 1982, 65).

Over time, the HRP included in its portfolio a much stronger social scientific component aimed at giving priority to "choice of contraception," "community studies," and "the roles of women and men and the influence of those roles on reproductive behavior" (WHO 1986, 121).[8] The HRP biennial report for 1992–93 clearly shows a shift toward a focus on the sociomedical conception of human reproduction that had materialized by the late 1980s in the formulation of the concept of "reproductive health," implying a focus on the "close relationship between family planning, health, and development, and the necessity to integrate family planning activities with those of maternal and child health" (WHO 1994, 5). The reference to maternal and child health is important, as this tied in with the WHO's long-standing efforts to integrate family planning programs within existing health structures instead of having single-purpose, vertical family planning programs outside established health services. In the HRP special biennial report for 1986–87, José Barzelatto (1988) had specified the "cornerstones of reproductive health" as family planning, maternal care, infant and child care, and control of sexually transmitted diseases (12). Already in the late 1980s, however, some key actors were trying to reengineer the evaluative criterion of the field so that their positions and their programs would not be hit by criticisms from economists about population growth being a neutral phenomenon and from health experts seeking to regain jurisdictional control over fertility matters as a question of health, not economics.

In 1987, two major international conferences were held on the topic of safe motherhood and maternal and child health. They were field-specific moves to counter and usurp the challenge from health professionals about the overarching goal of family planning programs. In this perspective, bringing in concerns about maternal and child health could counter criticisms of the top-down focus of family planning programs. The World Bank convened a conference in Nairobi on "Safe Motherhood" that discussed the interrelation between maternal health and family planning. The same year, the conference on Better Health for Women and Children through Family Planning, jointly organized by the WHO, UNICEF, UNFPA, and the IPPF, was also held in Nairobi. By the late 1980s, this had led to a growing recognition of the mutual benefits of maternal and child health and fertility control.[9] The rationale behind the Better Health Conference was thus defined in terms of the wide appeal of the health rationale and its concomitant potential to generate political support and increased funding for both health services and population control policies. As noted in a Population Council report,

> Since the health rationale for family planning is the only rationale which transcends religious controversy or political prejudice, asserting it as the preeminent rationale was seen as a means of uniting governments, organizations and individuals more firmly behind the family planning cause. . . . Launching a process which would raise family planning higher on the international public health agenda would, it was hoped, *generate new resources and political commitment and reinvigorate existing health and family planning programs.* (1987, 6)

These two conferences foreshadowed a significant reshuffling. The types of capital that could be converted into recognized claims about population policy in general and family planning programs in particular gradually changed, with health concerns becoming more significant relative to economic considerations. Key organizations in the field shifted or sought to reengineer the field's symbolic capital by making the economic rationale for family planning implicit, shifting to a focus on the individual-level benefits, especially in terms of health, of fertility regulation in the context of a more generalized reference to the benefits of stabilizing world population. In effect, this harked back to earlier references—significant in public debates on the topic—to the underlying Malthusian concern, now linked to environmental aspects as well.

Safeguarding Positions and Reengineering the Field

In 1977, Zeidenstein, the newly elected president of the Population Council, had observed that within the broader field of development, "population has generally been seen as a sectoral concern, with family planning as its primary component and with its own objectives, agencies programs and funding requirements" (307). While noting that this might be effective in controlling population growth, he argued, "The hard core of the population problem lies elsewhere . . . precisely in those situations in which requisite demand does not exist and cannot be generated by skillful application of red-triangle posters and puppet shows" (307). In thus identifying the motivational lacunae in existing policy, Zeidenstein advanced, in a different terminology, what the developing countries had been arguing at the Bucharest conference: the "motivational" dimension of fertility behavior that had become marginalized in the context of the governmental imperative of effectuating population control in a cost-effective manner.

Linked to this "motivational" or "developmental" focus was an orientation that had been growing in force since the late 1960s, as expressed in the fight for the legalization of abortion in the United States and for liberalizing abortion and divorce laws in Western Europe (Dixon-Mueller 1993). One specific expression of this reorientation within the Population Council is seen in the hiring of more female researchers and the attendant shift to research around the problem of "motivation" for family planning. For example, this effort saw the development of the concept of the "quality of care," later used as a platform for the development of a "reproductive health and rights" platform. Dunlop was instrumental in redirecting the funding to various pro-choice organizations in the United States through her collaboration with Rockefeller, who became a key figure in US politics of abortion (Critchlow 1999, 192–200; Dunlop 2010). Dunlop and Germain, together with Ruth Dixon-Mueller, Judith Bruce, and Beverly Winnikoff, worked for or through funding from the Population Council from the mid-1980s onward to effectuate a transformation of the field, seeking to shift the reference point and justification for fertility regulation by drawing on something akin to ethnographic authority—positioning themselves as representatives for and conveyors of the concerns and rights of women in the developing world regarding family planning programs.

Bruce, for example, initiated her discussion in "Implementing the User's Perspective" (1980) by arguing, "The individual's perspective and experience have often been viewed as discretionary and dispensable items, rather than as determining factors in the effectiveness of a birth planning programs" (29). The article criticized not only family planning programs but also the methodology and concepts applied in studies of family planning programs. The KAP studies and their successors—the World Fertility Survey, the Contraceptive Prevalence Surveys, and the Demographic and Health Surveys—constructed and collected data in a particular way, aimed at creating an objective reference for the viability of family planning programs. Writing in 1992, Dixon-Mueller and Germain—both central in shaping the agenda of the women's health movement—attacked the way in which demographers

had defined "unmet need" in terms motivated by demographic considerations with macrolevel population growth rather than with the concerns and
needs of individual women in the developing world:

> When a woman tells an interviewer that she is not practicing con-
> traception even though she does not want to get pregnant and is at
> some risk of doing so, she is said by some definition to have an unmet
> need for family planning. The "need" in this case is defined not by the
> woman herself, but by the researchers who deduce it from the appar-
> ent inconsistency between her contraceptive behavior and her stated
> reproductive preferences. (330)

More important for the formulation of the reproductive health approach, however, was the charge that the concept of "unmet need" should
be expanded to include women who used unsafe or unreliable contraceptives
and women with mistimed and unwanted pregnancies needing access to safe
abortion (Dixon-Mueller and Germain 1992, 333).

This attempt to broaden the definition of "unmet need" was important
because established methodologies and categories had been formulated to
address questions that assumed their relevance against the background of
a concern with population growth, not reproductive health (Halfon 2000,
211–12). It was a question of the "unmet need" for family planning, as measured by surveys serving as the market research for family planning. For
Bruce, establishing "the individual as the analytical focal point" had a clear
demographic rationale: in order to address the problem of discontinued use
of contraceptives (and make family planning programs for effective for reducing fertility rates), it was necessary to probe into why individuals failed
to use contraceptives and family planning services more consistently.

Reproductive health and rights soon came to form a more general label
for the attempt to establish a new policy approach driven by a set of goals
focused on the health and rights of individuals, particularly women. In essence, the apparent shift from "population control" to "reproductive health
and rights" was a move on the part of dominant actors in the field to shift
from "objective" to a kind of "ethnographic" reference point—from a focus on macrolevel data summarized through KAP studies and their link to
economic growth and to a focus on the individual user and the concerns
of women as categorized and explained by analysts with credentials in the
field. The advocates of a reproductive health approach—organized around
the rights and concerns of women—sought to appropriate a position of authority by claiming to speak more directly for and on behalf of women in

the developing world. Their efforts, targeted at a new "consensus" at the UN-organized Cairo conference in 1994, were in this perspective highly structured by the active forces in the field, with a commitment to the continuation of family planning programs: their goal was neither to abandon such programs nor to address population growth as such but rather to make the "individual user" the ultimate reference point for such efforts.

John Bongaarts, vice president of the Population Council and a renowned demographer, provided a central demographic rationale for accentuating the quality dimension of family planning programs and for supporting a focus on "reproductive health and rights." In an article published in *Science* in February 1994, at the height of the preparatory process for the Cairo conference, he argued that of the three causes of population growth (unwanted fertility, high desired family size, and population momentum), family planning programs attacked only the first, not the other two, although these two together explained more of the total population growth than the first. Addressing the two other causes would require programs aimed at changing what people saw as desired family size (which would mean addressing the "motivational" aspect or demand side of fertility behavior) and delaying early childbirth. That in turn pointed to the importance of investing in gender issues, in promoting girls' education, and generally working to change sociocultural norms for family size and timing of first births.

The US delegation to the Cairo conference was headed by Vice President Al Gore, known for his involvement in environmental issues. It is indicative of the importance of Bongaarts's demographically based call for a focus on other aspects than family planning for population control that Gore, having been briefed by Bongaarts in August 1994 (Bongaarts 2000), told reporters just prior to his departure for Cairo that a more "comprehensive and humane strategy" was needed. Measures to reduce population growth, Gore explained, would have to include a focus on girls' education, empowerment of women, and investments in work that generally "fosters women's health."[10]

An equally important demographic rationale for a move toward an approach centered on reproductive health and rights was presented in an article in *International Family Planning Perspectives* in March 1994. "Seeking Common Ground: Unmet Need and Demographic Goals" was written by three prominent figures: Steve Sinding, director of population sciences at the Rockefeller Foundation; John Ross of the Population Council; and Allan Rosenfield, dean of the School of Public Health at Columbia University. The authors aimed to transcend the established distinctions in the field, arguing that these could easily be overcome by simply focusing on "service" rather than "targets." They argued that "in addition to relieving the conflict over how to lower fertility, an emphasis on services instead of targets should help alleviate another prevailing tension, that between population and health programs" (26).

The link to a clear-cut demographic rationale for an expanded, more quality-oriented approach to fertility regulation provided by Bongaarts's analysis and by the work of the Sinding-Ross-Rosenfield trio was central to the support that this new policy approach was to receive from organizations like the UNFPA, whose rationale for existence was the presence of a population problem. In fact, the more general political mobilization around and advancement of this policy approach came to take on a far more overtly politicized form than had been the case in the formative phase of the policy field. In Donald Critchlow's (1999) interpretation, "The mobilization of grassroots groups meant that power shifted from elite interests, which had played a critical role in the shaping of family planning policy in the first three decades following the Second World War, to social movements organized on the community level" (185). As noted by Amy Higer (1997), feminist-oriented researchers, advocates, and foundation officials gradually came to gain influence in policy circles after the mid-1980s (see also Hodgson and Watkins 1997, 497–98). It was on this basis that efforts to formulate and advance a comprehensive policy approach under the heading of reproductive health and rights began to gain momentum.

These interpretations ignore the fact that the mobilization of grassroots groups was predicated on a field-specific move to shift the register from macrolevel data to an image of the individual endowed with rights within which the continuation of existing practice—family planning aimed at reducing population growth—could be legitimized. That is, the actors involved in the push for reproductive health and rights were all professionals in the sense that I use it here—with credentials allowing them access to international arenas to speak on behalf of others. And some of these actors—those with contacts within established institutions—were instrumental in forging the very categories through which such a "voice" was given to new types of actors organized by the International Women's Health Coalition.

In January 1994, 215 women's health advocates from seventy-nine countries met in Rio de Janeiro to formulate a common position. Referred to as the "feminist prepcom," the meeting represented a central arena for the formulation of a common position ahead of the Cairo conference. It testifies to the primacy of positions in investing claims with authority that those with credentials from the very same organizations that had for decades designed and administered the types of policies now to be attacked, like the IPPF and the Population Council, defined the categories through which these women's groups were to mobilize to introduce new language on population policy at the Cairo conference. The two key figures in this effort, Dunlop and Germain, had set up the International Women's Health Coalition, with initial funding from Rockefeller, in an effort to get domestic groups in the US interested in international matters. They could operate at the top echelons of the Population Council and at the IPPF and UNFPA by virtue of the credentials they had already established and could marshal that capital to forge a new agenda, shifting the register of justification within this field to the rights-endowed individual.

According to the Rio Statement that resulted from the conference, the coalition sought to "provide a forum where women could search for and identify commonalities on reproductive health and justice" (International Women's Health Coalition and Cidadania, Estudos, Pesquisa, Informação, Ação 1994, 4). It goes on to note,

> The participants strongly voiced their opposition to population policies intended to control the fertility of women and that do not address their basic right to secure livelihood, freedom from poverty and oppression; or do not respect their rights to free, informed choice or to adequate health care; that whether such policies are pro- or anti-natalist, they are often coercive, treat women as objects, not subjects, and that in the context of such policies, low fertility does not result in alleviating poverty. (4)

While the Cairo conference has been hailed as a "paradigm shift," the document it produced reflects a sustained focus on population control, albeit in subdued language. Principle 4 of the Programme of Action notes, "Advancing gender equality and equity and the empowerment of women, and the elimination of all kinds of violence against women, and ensuring women's ability to control their own fertility, are cornerstones of population and development-related programs" (UN 1995, 9). Paragraph 3.16 of the section on "Population Growth, Sustained Economic Growth, and Poverty" places the individual subject, endowed with rights, clearly in the context of efforts to reduce population growth:

> *Particular attention is to be given to the socio-economic improvement of poor women in developed and developing countries.* As women are generally the poorest of the poor and at the same time key actors in the development process, eliminating social, cultural, political and economic discrimination against women is a *prerequisite* of eradicat-

ing poverty, promoting sustained economic growth in the context of
sustainable development . . . , and achieving balance between population and available resources and sustainable patterns of consumption
and production. (14)

Conclusion

In the 1950s and 1960s, population governance became established as a
transnational field. The boundaries and internal hierarchy of that field was
shaped by the theory of demographic transition. The content of this theory
was itself the outcome of a series of moves aimed at gaining recognition from
actors with resources to initiate action programs. In time, these categories,
key among which were the distinctions between means and motives and
between economics and health, assumed status as second nature and came to
organize the field and define its specific stakes for superordinate and subordinate actors alike. The intergovernmental conferences—Bucharest, Mexico
City, and Cairo—all brought new dynamics to the field by making it easier
to convert capital from the outside to bear on debates within it. While previous practices continued basically unabated, these UN conferences did affect
the terms of debate and the relative purchase of field-specific forms of capital.
The establishment of reproductive health and rights approach at the Cairo
conference constituted a change of rhetoric and justification as well as partly
of the organization of family planning services. But this was also a transformation very much orchestrated by the same organizations—the Population
Council, the IPPF, and the UNFPA—that had dominated the field since its
inception. Actors with access to and contacts in these organizations—key
among them Joan Dunlop and Adrienne Germain—were in positions to
appropriate and construct new categories through which to establish a new
source of authority anchored in the claim to be speaking on behalf of and
representing the interests and concerns of women endowed with rights and
health concerns. The structuring force of the categories that helped shape the
field and that determined its boundaries and topography cannot be captured
by analyses that take for granted the positions of actors and their strategies.
Having here focused on the contents of these categories and their effects on
the relations between actors—the subordination of health professionals, for
example—and these actors' search for recognition for their distinctive view
of fertility regulation, it has been possible to capture the stability and the
changes in the relations of authority among those professionals with a stake
in governing for and on behalf of others.

Conclusion

Fields and the Study of Global Governance

What matters most in shaping the contents of global governance? One way to answer this question is to identify which states are dominant within an anarchic or competitive world and then see which constellation of interests ultimately prevails. This is the traditional approach within IR theory: the contents of global governance are an effect of and are explained by the distribution of power and the competitive interaction between (primarily) states, where analysts disagree, for example, on relative versus absolute gains (Keohane and Martin 1995; Mearsheimer 1994) or whether world politics is best understood through the lens of a logic of consequences, appropriateness, or arguing (Checkel and Zürn 2005; March and Olsen 1998; Risse 2001). Another way to go about this is to assume what traditional IR theory investigates—namely, cooperation—and to analyze, as in the literature on global governance, which types of actors are dominant in different issue areas. Here, too, the *explanandum* is which types of actors are most powerful and whether some of these are able to stabilize their domination (authority) over time.

In both of these approaches, the contents of governance efforts figure primarily as arenas for observation, either as to state power and interests or about the authority or strategies of nonstate actors. It matters little for the analysis whether the empirical focus is on security, trade, or human rights: the theoretical tools are honed to answer questions about the conditions under which states can and do cooperate, or—in the case of analysts of global governance—the researcher assumes cooperation and analyzes the power of nonstate actors relative to that of states. I argue for a shift in perspective where the emergence, institutionalization, and changes in the contents of governance efforts are made the object rather than the arena of analysis. Global governance here becomes an interdependent system in which various actors compete to define what is to be governed, how, and why. By way of conclusion, I discuss some of the implications of this conceptualization.

Fields and Institutional Forms

I have thus far avoided taking on the question of how to conceptualize the state. For Bourdieu, the state has a monopoly of symbolic violence, thereby determining the exchange rates and relations between fields (Bourdieu 1994, 3–5). A more central question is therefore whether it makes sense to think of fields in a social space where there is no overarching authority, no single actor that monopolizes the means of symbolic violence. There is certainly a sense in which fields are nested, where some set the terms for the functioning of others. If we think about fields within a national frame of reference, the state can be said to monopolize symbolic capital and to constitute a "field of power" that subordinates other fields. But fields need not be anchored or held together by the institutional form of the state. It should be recalled that Bourdieu in part took his cues from Weber's discussion of the differentiation of value spheres in formulating the concept of field. Moreover, Bourdieu's own writings on the state draw on Durkheim's idea of state formation as a process where some group of actors differentiate themselves from society by seizing control over certain resources. Bourdieu (1994) refers, for example, to the role of jurists in appropriating and codifying juridical capital as symbolic capital, thereby giving the state a particular bureaucratic form (11). As conceived here, however, fields are not so much subordinated to and thus dependent on the institutional framework of the state. Rather, it is organized around and derives its form from particular objects of governance, and it is the sociogenesis of these objects that has to be explored in order to understand who has authority and why, and how boundaries and hierarchies are established. It is therefore an empirical question how and with what effects claims to represent a state have purchase on the functioning of specific field. Consider, in this context, Richard Ashley's (1984) argument to the effect that "To have power, an agent must first secure its recognition as an agent capable of having power, and, to do that, it must first demonstrate its competence in terms of the collective and co-reflective structures . . . by which the community confers meaning and organizes collective expectations" (259). Surely, diplomats are formally recognized as representatives of states and as such their status as competent actors is secured by virtue of established legal and political practice. Nonetheless, the degree to which diplomats are recognized as having power or authority on any given object depends to a considerable degree on the contents of the field-specific cognitive structures or classificatory schemes that define that social space, which are in turn the outcome of historical struggles between professional actors that are often transnational or international in character. In short, the claim to represent the state is but one (significant) dimension of a larger set of classificatory schemes within which competence and authority is determined (Sending, Pouliot, and Neumann 2015).

The upshot of this is that we should be attentive not so much to whether an actor represents a state or some other type of actor, but rather to the shared registers within which any type of actor can possibly succeed in claiming competence on what is to be governed, how, and why. As we have seen, this varies considerably both between fields and within fields over time: We saw in chapters 2 and 3 that a field of international rule did emerge with the League of Nations and subsequently with the United Nations. This was, and remains, a heterodox field, characterized by contestation over what the field is about. This field is not, however, an international counterpart to what Bourdieu termed the "field of power"—a meta field in which the state is the ultimate arbiter over the relative importance of different types of capital and so on. Rather, the field of international rule should be understood as organized around particular objects of governing, the character of which has changed over time: In the interwar years, the League initially established itself in a position of authority vis a vis states in handling how minorities should be governed. From the 1950s onwards, the UN Secretariat established a similar level of authority in managing friction between great powers, as in the UNEF operation after the Suez crisis, and in managing the transition from colonial rule to independence, as in the ONUC operations in the 1960s. In chapters 4 and 5, by contrast, we saw that academic credentials were important, because the field had been constructed around a particular theoretical formulation that was itself a product of demographers' search for recognition from actors with resources to transform theoretical propositions into action programs. As this field became institutionalized through transnational rather than international channels, the premium placed on knowledge production was higher than any other type of capital, including that of diplomatic representation. Here, state representatives had little say on the functioning of the field. It was only when the UN organized intergovernmental conferences—in 1974, 1984, and 1994— that the otherwise autonomous logic of the field was disrupted, increasing the relative importance of diplomats qua agents of states.

Global Governance as a System of Professional Competition

One virtue of approaching global governance and world politics more generally in terms of fields is that the competition between professional groups moves center stage as explanation of the contents of governance objects. This, in turn, opens up for more in-depth explorations of how the identity of governance objects and governance subjects is endogenous to the process whereby the latter seeks to establish or maintain a position of authority over the former. The definition or meaning of a distinct object of governance should therefore not be assumed to have intrinsic attributes that are subsequently identified and acted on. Rather, governance objects—security, climate, reproduction, trade, migration, and the like—emerge with distinct attributes and are differentiated from other objects of governance through the competition between different actors or subjects of governance to establish some level of authority to govern them (Seabrooke 2014). For Abbott (2005), for example, the process of constructing a relationship between a governance subject (actor) and a governance object—what he calls "tasks"—is primary in shaping their respective identities: "Creating a psychiatric approach to shell shock in World War I . . . redefined who psychiatrists were and what shell shock was more than it defined a relation between a pre-existing group and a given task" (250). The preceding chapters have demonstrated how the identity and characteristics of the actors changed over time precisely as a result of the evolution of the field in which they operated: US demographers initially struggled to become recognized as a scientific discipline, then became involved managing a global push for population control, and were subsequently forced to reorient themselves to invest in reproductive health. Similarly, the identity of international civil servants changed significantly as the meaning of the realm over which they claimed authority—the international—changed over time from a model of diplomatic mediator to one engaged in social engineering.

The competition over positions of authority to construct and act on the world also suggests that we as analysts should move away from a primary focus on the (ontological point) about the construction of social reality, showing how state perceptions, behavior, and interests are shaped by knowledge claims, and instead explore the (epistemological point) about the social (and competitive) construction of this knowledge (Guzzini 2000, 160). If the categories through which social reality is made intelligible and manageable for us are bound up with professional competition, then they have significant consequences for how we should analyze global governance qua political debates about how to govern.

The challenge becomes one of treating professional actors' analytical categories as practice categories: professional actors compete with others to be recognized as authoritative and in the process produce and deploy technical terms and categories since there is generally a premium on an appearance of analytical precision. Their formulation and use are to be understood with reference to the particular contest, within particular fields, to establish authority and control over specific tasks or jurisdictions (Abbott 1988). This, in turn, has bearing on our understanding of the character of debates that is claimed to accord a level of legitimacy to global governance. To the extent that *debates* about the contents of global governance are dominated by technical terms in the hands of professional groups, it calls into question the alleged publicness and legitimacy of such debates and of global governance more generally (Eriksen and Sending 2013).

Publicness and Representation

There is a glaring omission in this book that in one sense reflects the neglect of the question of publicness in studies of global governance: there are no—or very few—reference(s) to those actors who are the targets of either population control or peacebuilding efforts. Were women in developing countries—the targets of family planning programs—not part of the field of population? Are those who live in South Sudan or the Democratic Republic of Congo not part of the field of peacebuilding? The ostensible benefactors of these governing practices should clearly be seen as part of these fields inasmuch as they are subject to their logic. I have opted to focus on professionals to analyze the competition for authority, but there are costs to such a choice. Even in the analysis in chapter 5, focused on the criticism of family planning by women's groups, those at the receiving end of these efforts did not figure in the analysis other than as examples and illustrations used by researchers and professional advocacy groups. Similarly, the citizens of those countries where peacebuilding efforts take place were not part of the analysis in chapter 3. In both cases, those subject to the governing practices in both fields only figured through intermediaries who claimed to speak on behalf of these actors and in so doing appropriated a distinct type of capital.

While there are differences across fields, the ones under study here are marked by a distinct hierarchical ordering in which those who are affected by decisions about what is to be governed, how, and why are not part of and arguably are not duly represented in these debates. These actors are represented by professionals who invoke their experiences, concerns, and interests and can marshal and package such claims to representation as a form of capital to use in a particular field (Hopgood 2009). As discussed in chapter 2, claims to representation can be powerful, as they entail a potentially effective instantiation of successful presentation of one's "private" or subjective interests as "public" ones in which the claim to represent a particular group can help conceal the particular interests at stake and present them as objective, natural, or universal. This is so because the coherence and identity of any group being presented by some actor is a product of the claims made by the representer rather than vice versa (Bourdieu 1991, 223; 2004).

For Hobbes, the fear and the impossibility of knowing the intention of others in a state of nature prompts actors to make a covenant to establish an overarching, sovereign, authority that represents the collective will of and is thereby authorized by those who agree to establish such authority (Holland 2010; see also Orford 2011). The sovereign is thus "in authority," having been vested with sovereignty by virtue of the contract established to substitute procedural agreement for lack of the possibility of substantive agreement. But the trick involved in claims to representation is that it is possible to conceal the active and potentially productive force of defining what is to be represented in this rather than that way: it is possible to invoke the ideal of popular sovereignty—that authority to govern is delegated from those over whom it is exercised—to construct authority that is not delegated.

Students of the modern state know this all too well. The modern state is surely in authority by virtue of the rules and procedures established to identify and select an occupant of such a position rather than by the contents of the commands it issues. At the same time, the modern state is also actively involved in the construction and disciplining of a shared framework within which the representatives of the state can be recognized as more competent and skilled in defining the categories within which actors' very identity and interests are formed. For this reason, the modern state appears as both independent of and standing somehow above society as well as flowing from it, representing it (see Mitchell 1991).

The very same dynamic is on display in global governance. Those who compete for and may prevail with authority within distinct fields of global governance invariably claim to speak in the name of and to represent broader groups. Inasmuch as these actors are recognized by others who are part of the field qua sharing an interest in and investing in it, they develop and advance categories that have consequences for and become authoritative for the very groups on whose behalf these actors claim (merely) to speak.

This has implications also for how we think about claims to distinctively global authority. Both Stephen Hopgood and Jens Bartelson suggest that authority beyond the state rest on claims to noncontingent values or principles. For Bartelson, the lack of an Archimedean anchor for international authority generates a problem, for it pushes would-be "governors" to ground authority in subject's voluntary submission to it:

> The true believers in global governance. . . . find themselves in a predicament not unlike that of those in the past who wanted to defend imperial authority, but who could no longer point upwards in the search for legitimacy, and were therefore faced with the impossible task of explaining why people should voluntarily subject themselves to a political authority over which they have no real control. (Bartelson 2009, 179)

Similarly, Hopgood argues—building on Simmel—that there is a tension between claiming authority with reference to noncontingent principles applicable everywhere, advanced and defined by cosmopolitans that work (for example) for international organizations, and the "claims to national and ethnic loyalty, to historical cultural traditions." The former is thin, associated with the "stranger," the latter is thick and linked to belonging and substantive identities:

> by transcending the subjectivity of thick life modern strangers take unto themselves the authority of the view from nowhere. In this way they facilitate their integration into all communities as strangers with an objective view superior to all subjective ones. The portal for this is "humanity." . . . To recognize the stranger is no longer in the gift of the host community. It is now a claim made by the stranger him- or herself, legitimized in the language of . . . "the international community" and "the community of mankind." Our cosmopolitans stand in the same relation of alienation to all thick social identities. (Hopgood 2009, 238)

There is something profoundly important in these arguments. And yet, both seem to imply that the expansion of international authority is (necessarily) grounded in a set of non-contingent principles that is construed as outside society. But authority need not, as I have tried to show here, be understood in this way, since it rests on a continual search for recognition within always already hierarchically organized social spaces: claims to represent the international—as we saw in chapters 2 and 3—can be effective because they are presented as—and may be recognized as—empirical (contingent) and concrete qua expression of a pre-constituted group's interests and identity, and yet contain significant normative elements that move beyond and in fact help define and constitute those very interests. Similarly, as detailed in chapters 4 and 5, the authority to define and act on reproductive behavior on a global scale emerged very much through how elite groups in both developed and developing countries presented their particular interests as universal ones and constructed a contingent and shifting rather than noncontingent register (economic growth and reproductive health) against which others had to refer to be seen as competent and relevant.

Misrecognition and Ontological Costs

The misrecognition that is potentially involved in claims to representation—via scientific knowledge production, moral values, or simply "humanity"—opens up a more fundamental question about the social and political costs of some actors being in a position not only to have authority to instruct but also to construct the categories by which others are compelled to refer for recognition. For Patchen Markell (2003), a full appreciation of the dynamics of misrecognition is to be gained by first reflecting on the ontological features of social life. It is, he claims, drawing on Hannah Arendt, fundamentally contingent, complex and open-ended, impossible to capture, control, and plan (4–5). Those actors who seek and achieve positions of authority to construct categories through which others see and act in the world achieve a semblance of "sovereign agency" by virtue of being able to establish categories that transfer the costs of the contingency and unpredictability of life disproportionately onto others: US elites saw a problem of global population growth and a problem on the horizon in the competition with the Soviet Union. In defining population growth as a problem and devising an apparent solution, these actors achieved a semblance of sovereign agency, having thus ordered the world and addressed it while the effects of this effort are borne by others. Markell argues that "relations of social and political subordination" can be seen as "ways of patterning and arranging the world that allow some people and groups to enjoy a semblance of sovereign agency at others' expense" (5). The governing structures I have analyzed in this book emerge in this light as also harboring a systematic reallocation of risks and contingency. That is, governing practices, established through competitive struggles for authority by some actors claiming to represent others—and thereby involved in defining the identity of those whom they claim to represent—can "organize the human world in ways that make it possible for certain people to enjoy an imperfect simulation of the invulnerability they desire, leaving others to bear a disproportionate share of the costs and burdens in social life" (22). This feature of global governance—of governing more generally—implies that we should try to unpack and critically examine which actors pay the price for the semblance of control and sovereign agency on the part of those who construct categories through which to govern.

Notes

1. This is similar to a "competence model," where recognition from relevant others is given priority in assessing an actor's power: what matters is therefore not in the first instance the general resources (economic and military resources, say) that an actor can use but which resources are regarded as relevant and significant within any particular settings. See Ashley 1984, 259–60.

Chapter 1

1. Other critics of the epistemic communities approach have argued that it fails to differentiate among types of knowledge Dimitrov (2003); that it overlooks the "disciplinary power" of knowledge (Litfin 1994), that the material basis of knowledge is not accounted for (Bieler 2001); that it ignores how "knowledge-brokers" manipulate scientifically established facts to further specific goals (Eriksson and Sundelius 2005); and that it fails to grasp the political conditioning of knowledge-based policy idea (Bernstein 2001). Adopting a very different approach, Lidskog and Sundqvist (2002, 84) see the interplay between knowledge and politics as one of evolution, where "scientific knowledge and the political order are shaping each other through an inter-dependent process of evolution." Theirs is a functional argument where it is unclear who effectuates the "fit" between knowledge claims and the broader political order. The concept of episteme advanced by Adler and Bernstein (2005) is slightly different. An episteme is concerned with the intersubjective background knowledge—the "bubble"—within which and from which actors see the world and act in it (295–96). Thus, it can identify mutually constitutive structures (of liberalism as a political project and knowledge production linked to its advancement), but it is not fine-grained enough to capture how different actors may produce and use different knowledge claims in seeking to become recognized as authoritative in the eyes of policymakers.

2. Certainly, some of this variation can be attributed to the unity of an IO's expertise. The IMF and the World Bank, for example, are widely seen as authoritative in

large part because of the relative homogeneity and general status of the economic expertise of their staff (Broome and Seabrooke 2007; Chwieroth 2008).

3. Avant, Finnemore, and Sell (2010) also list moral authority—or what they call "principled authority"—as one of many sources of authority of "global governors." They note, "NGOs often benefit from an aura of moral authority because of this perceived altruism" but are careful to stress that moral authority can only function among those who already share the moral values that are being claimed for that position of authority. As I explore later, this seems to limit the purchase of having moral authority, since such authority is over those who already agree with such advocacy groups, not the targets of their advocacy.

4. For a good discussion of Cassirer's philosophy of symbolic forms, see Krois 1987.

Chapter 2

1. For an important analysis along such lines from which I draw inspiration, see Ashley 1984, 66–75.

2. See http://www.un.org/Depts/dhl/dag/time1955.htm.

3. See www.un.org/sg/sg_role.shtml. Accessed June 2014.

Chapter 3

1. I refer to it as *peacebuilding* in order to highlight that present-day operations managed by the Department of Peacekeeping Operations and the Department of Field Support within the UN Secretariat go well beyond the so-called traditional deployment of troops to secure a peace agreement or an armistice between two parties. It includes protection of civilians, electoral monitoring, establishing rule of law, securing compliance with human rights, and so on. It amounts to "state building" in that the tasks and objectives of these operations and the work done by other UN agencies, the World Bank, and NGOs in tandem or parallel with the UN Secretariat cover a whole array of activities directed at rebuilding and transforming the state in question.

2. Interview, DPKO official, January 2011.

3. Interview, diplomat at Indian Mission, January 2012.

4. Telephone interview, official from mission of a NAM country. For reasons of anonymity, the diplomat wanted me not to identify nationality.

5. Interview, diplomat at Norwegian mission, New York, November 2010.

6. Interview, diplomat at French mission, New York, November 2010.

7. Author's field notes, Juba, October 2010.

8. Interview, former UNMIS official, Oslo, March 2012; interview, diplomat formerly stationed in Pakistan and East Jerusalem, Oslo, April 2012.

9. Interview, former UNHCR official, Oslo, April 2012.

10. Interview, former UNMIL official, New York, January 2012.

11. Interview, UNHCR official, Juba, October 2010.

12. Interview, UNMIL officer, Monrovia, 2008.

13. Ibid.

14. Telephone interview, former DPKO official, November 20, 2011.

15. Personal communication, former DPKO official, May 2012.

16. This is based on an—admittedly limited—analysis of LinkedIn profiles of more than fifty international civil servants, divided equally between Civil Affairs and Political Affairs positions as reported in their respective CVs, with their current position as of June 2013 as the basis for categorization.

17. Interview, former UNMIL official, Civil Affairs, New York, January 20, 2012.

18. Telephone interview, UNMIL official, Monrovia, February 2012.

19. Interview, former UNMIL official, New York, January 2012.

20. Interview, former UNMIS official, Oslo, March 2012.

21. I use *peacebuilders* as shorthand for external or international actors involved in postconflict reconstruction of some sort, notably through UN peacekeeping operations but also through other UN entities and other international organizations (World Bank). This should also include nongovernmental organizations, but I focus here mainly on UN actors.

Chapter 4

1. The 1873 Comstock Law criminalized the sale or distribution of materials that could be used for contraception.

2. For an excellent analysis of variation between countries in how the same scientific discipline is anchored or configured in society, see Fourcade 2009, which shows how economics is constituted differently in France, the UK, and the US. For example, in France, proximity to policymakers is important for the validation of knowledge qua knowledge, whereas in the US, the market is more important.

3. An earlier statement along the same lines is found in Ross 1927.

4. Nevertheless, Notestein carried the most weight in determining which issues were to be addressed and what individuals should be invited. See McLean 1952c.

Chapter 5

1. Resolution XVIII on the Human Rights Aspects of Family Planning stated in its operative paragraph 3, "Couples have a basic human right to decide freely and responsibly on the number and spacing of their children and a right to adequate education and information in this respect" (Final Act of the International Conference on Human Rights. U.N. Doc. A/CONF. 32/41, p. 15).

2. For other references and analyses of the central role of the KAP studies in providing the grounds for action programs, see Casterline and Sinding 2000; Mauldin 1965; Stycos 1964; Warwick 1983, 1994.

3. The Alan Guttmacher Institute was first established in 1968 as the Center for Family Planning Program Development and was renamed after Guttmacher's death in 1974. Guttmacher was president of the Planned Parenthood Federation of America from 1964 to 1974.

4. For other contributions to this debate, see Hauser 1969; Rosenfield 1976.

5. For a review of the evolution of these debates, see Sinding 2000; see also Hodgson 1988.

6. Pierre Padervand, "Realistic Approaches to the Acceptance of Family Planning in Africa," John D. Rockefeller III files (unprocessed), 281 n. 104. Rockefeller Archive Center.

7. As reports on the major focus and priorities of research, these biennial reports of the WHO, when used comparatively, provide insights about changes over time in the direction of and rationale for various research projects.

8. The report notes that the HRP was either supporting or monitoring thirty such research projects.

9. Representative contributions include Alauddin 1986; Chen et al. 1983; Fortney 1987; Omran 1987; Omran, Standley, and Azar 1976.

10. Transcript of remarks by Vice President Al Gore, National Press Club, Washington, DC, August 25, 1994. Reprinted in Al Gore "The Rapid Growth of the Human Population: Sustainable Economic Growth," *Vital Speeches of the Day*, Vol. 60, no. 24, October 1, 741–45.

Bibliography

Abbott, Andrew. 1988. *The System of Professions.* Chicago: University of Chicago Press.

Abbott, Andrew. 2005. "Linked Ecologies: States and Universities as Environments for Professions." *Sociological Theory* 23 (2): 245–74.

Abrahamsen, Rita, and Michael C. Williams. 2010. *Security beyond the State: Private Security in International Politics.* Cambridge: Cambridge University Press.

Abrams, Irwin. 1957. "The Emergence of the International Law Societies." *Review of Politics* 19 (3): 361–80.

Adler, Emanuel. 1992. "The Emergence of Cooperation: National Epistemic Communities and the International Evolution of the Idea of Nuclear Arms Control." *International Organization* 46 (1): 101–45.

Adler, Emanuel. 2005. *Communitarian International Relations: The Epistemic Foundations of International Relations.* New York: Routledge.

Adler, Emanuel, and Steven Bernstein. 2005. "Knowledge in Power: The Epistemic Construction of Global Governance." In *Power In Global Governance,* edited by Michael Barnett and Raymond Duvall. New York: Cambridge University Press.

Adler-Nissen, Rebecca. 2014. "Symbolic Power in European Diplomacy: The Struggle between National Foreign Services and the EU's External Action Service." *Review of International Studies* 40 (4): 657–81.

Ahluwalia, Sanjam. 2007. *Reproductive Restraints: Birth Control in India, 1877–1947.* Urbana: University of Illinois Press.

Alauddin, Mohammad. 1986. "Maternal Mortality in Rural Bangladesh: The Tangail District." *Studies in Family Planning* 17 (1): 13–21.

Alvarez, José E. 2002. "The WTO as Linkage Machine." *American Journal of International Law* 96 (146): 146–58.

Anghie, Antony. 2006. "The Evolution of International Law: Colonial and Postcolonial Realities." *Third World Quarterly* 27 (5): 739–53.

Ashley, Richard K. 1984. "The Poverty of Neorealism." *International Organization* 38 (2): 225–86.

Autesserre, Séverine. 2010. *The Trouble with the Congo: Local Violence and the Failure of International Peacebuilding.* Cambridge: Cambridge University Press.

Avant, Deborah Denise, Martha Finnemore, and Susan K Sell. 2010. *Who Governs the Globe?* Cambridge: Cambridge University Press.

Bain, William. 2003. "The Political Theory of Trusteeship and the Twilight of International Equality." *International Relations* 17 (1): 59–77.

Balfour, M., Roger F. Evans, Frank W. Notestein, and Irene B. Taeuber. 1950. *Public Health and Demography in the Far East*. New York: Rockefeller Foundation.

Barnett, Michael. 1995. "The New United Nations Politics of Peace: From Juridical Sovereignty to Empirical Sovereignty." *Global Governance* 1 (1): 79–97.

Barnett, Michael, and Martha Finnemore. 2004. *Rules of the World: International Organizations in Global Politics*. Ithaca: Cornell University Press.

Bartelson, Jens. 1995. *A Genealogy of Sovereignty*. Cambridge: Cambridge University Press.

Bartelson, Jens. 2009. *Visions of World Community*. Cambridge: Cambridge University Press.

Barzelatto, José. 1988. "Continuity and Change." In *Research in Human Reproduction: Biennial Report of 1986–87*, edited by E. Diczfalusy, P. D. Griffin, and J. Khanna. Geneva: WHO.

Bentham, Jeremy. 1789/1988. *The Principles of Morals and Legislation*. New York: Prometheus.

Berelson, Bernard. 1969. "Beyond Family Planning." *Studies in Family Planning* 1 (38): 1–16.

Bernstein, Steven. 2001. *The Compromise of Liberal Environmentalism*. New York: Columbia University Press.

Bernstein, Steven, and Benjamin Cashore. 2007. "Can Non-State Global Governance Be Legitimate? An Analytical Framework." *Regulation and Governance* 1 (4): 347–71.

Best, Geoffrey. 1999. "Peace Conferences and the Century of Total War: The 1899 Hague Conference and What Came After." *International Affairs* 75 (3): 619–34.

Beyer, Cornelia. 2007. "Non-Governmental Organizations as Motors of Change." *Government and Opposition* 42 (4): 513–35.

Bhuta, Nehal. 2008. "Against State-Building." *Constellations* 15 (4): 517–42.

Bhuta, Nehal. 2012. "Governmentalizing Sovereignty: Indexes of State Fragility and the Calculability of Political Order." In *Governance by Indicators: Global Power through Quantification and Rankings*, edited by Kevin Davis, Angelina Fisher, Benedict Kingsbury, and Sally Engle Merry. Oxford: Oxford University Press.

Bieler, Andreas. 2001. "Questioning Cognitivism and Constructivism in IR Theory: Reflections on the Material Structure of Ideas." *Politics* 21 (2): 93–100.

Biersteker, Thomas. 1992. "The 'Triumph' of Neoclassical Economics in the Developing World: Policy Convergence and Bases of Governance in the International Economic Order." In *Governance without Government: Order and Change in World Politics*, edited by James Rosenau and Ernst-Otto Czempiel. Cambridge: Cambridge University Press.

Biersteker, Thomas J. 2012. "State, Sovereignty, and Territory." In *Handbook of International Relations*, edited by Walter Carlsnaes, Thomas Risse, and Beth A. Simmons. London: Sage.

Bigo, Didier, ed. 2007. *The Field of the EU Internal Security Agencies*. Paris: L'Harmattan.

Bigo, Didier. 2011. "Pierre Bourdieu and International Relations: Power of Practices, Practices of Power." *International Political Sociology* 5 (3): 225–58.

Blau, Peter M. 1963. "Critical Remarks on Weber's Theory of Authority." *American Political Science Review* 57 (2): 305–16.

Bogue, Donald T. 1966. "Family Planning Research: An Outline of the Field." In *Family Planning and Population Programs*, edited by Bernard Berelson. Chicago: University of Chicago Press.

Bongaarts, John. 1994. "Population Policy Options in the Developing World." *Science* 263: 771–76.

Bongaarts, John. 2000. Personal communication, April 4.

Boudreau, Frank G. 1941. *Program of the Division of Research, 1928–1940*. New York: Milbank Memorial Fund.

Boulding, Kenneth E. 1964. *The Meaning of the Twentieth Century: The Great Transition*. New York: Harper and Row.

Bourdieu, Pierre. 1984. *Distinction: A Social Critique of the Judgement of Taste*. Cambridge: Harvard University Press.

Bourdieu, Pierre. 1985. "The Social Space and the Genesis of Groups." *Theory and Society* 14 (6): 723–44.

Bourdieu, Pierre. 1990a. *In Other Words: Essays Towards a Reflexive Sociology*. Stanford: Stanford University Press.

Bourdieu, Pierre. 1990b. *The Logic of Practice*. Stanford: Stanford University Press.

Bourdieu, Pierre. 1990c. "Social Space and Symbolic Power." In *In Other Words: Essays Towards a Reflexive Sociology*. Stanford: Stanford University Press.

Bourdieu, Pierre. 1991. *Language and Symbolic Power*. Cambridge: Polity Press.

Bourdieu, Pierre. 1998. *Practical Reason: On the theory of Action*. Stanford, CA: Stanford University Press.

Bourdieu, Pierre. 1999. "Rethinking the State: Genesis and Structure of the Bureaucratic Field." In *State/Culture: State-Formation after the Cultural Turn*, edited by George Steinmetz. Ithaca: Cornell University Press.

Bourdieu, Pierre. 2000. *Pascalian Meditations*. Cambridge: Polity.

Bourdieu, Pierre. 2004. "The Mystery of the Ministry: From Particular Wills to the General Will." *Constellations* 11 (1): 37–43.

Bourdieu, Pierre, and Richard Nice. 1980. "The Production of Belief: Contribution to an Economy of Symbolic Goods." *Media, Culture, and Society* 2 (3): 261–93.

Bourdieu, Pierre, and Löic Wacquant. 1992. *An Invitation to Reflexive Sociology*. Chicago: University of Chicago Press.

Bourdieu, Pierre, Löic Wacquant, and Samar Farage. 1994. "Rethinking the State: Genesis and Structure of the Bureaucratic Field." *Sociological Theory* 12 (1): 1–18.

Bravo, Giuliano Ferrari. 1979. "National and International Trusteeship: Some Notes on UN Intervention in the System of Chapters XII and XIII of the Charter." *Africa* 34 (4): 391–416.

Broome, Andre, and Leonard Seabrooke. 2007. "Seeing Like the IMF: Institutional Change in Small Open Economies." *Review of International Political Economy* 14 (4): 576–601.

Bruce, Judith. 1980. "Implementing the User's Perspective." *Studies in Family Planning* 11 (1): 29–34.

Bruce, Judith. 1990. "Fundamental Elements of the Quality of Care: A Simple Framework." *Studies in Family Planning* 21 (2): 61–96.

Buck-Morss, Susan. 2009. *Hegel, Haiti, and Universal History.* Pittsburgh: University of Pittsburgh Press.

Bugge, Lars. 2007. "Struktur, Relasjon, Formidling: Noen momenter i en materialistisk sosiologi." PhD diss., University of Oslo.

Caldwell, John, and Pat Caldwell. 1986. *Limiting Population Growth and the Ford Foundation Contribution.* London: Pinters.

Candau, M. G. 1966. "Programme Activities in the Health Aspects of World Population Which Might Be Developed by WHO." In *World Health Assembly—Committee on Programme and Budget.* Geneva: WHO.

Carpenter, Charli R. 2010. "Governing the Global Agenda: 'Gatekeepers' and 'Issue Adoption' in Transnational Advocacy Networks." In *Who Governs the Globe?*, edited by Martha Finnemore, Deborah D. Avant, and Susan Sell. Cambridge: Cambridge University Press.

Carr-Saunders, Alexander Morris. 1922. *The Population Problem: A Study in Human Evolution.* Oxford: Clarendon.

Casterline, John B., and Steven W. Sinding. 2000. "Unmet Need for Family Planning in Developing Countries and Implications for Population Policy." *Population and Development Review* 26 (4): 691–723.

Chatterjee, Partha. 1993. *The Nation and Its Fragments: Colonial and Postcolonial Histories.* Princeton: Princeton University Press.

Chen, Lincoln C. Makhlisur Rahman, Stan D'Souza, J. Chakraborty, and A. M. Sardar. 1983. "Mortality Impact of an MCH-FP Program in Matlab, Bangladesh." *Studies in Family Planning* 14 (8–9): 199–209.

Chwieroth, Jeffrey. 2008. "Normative Change 'from Within': The International Monetary Fund's Approach to Capital Account Liberalization." *International Studies Quarterly* 52 (1): 129–58.

Cohen, Antonin. 2011. "Bourdieu Hits Brussels: The Genesis and Structure of the European Field of Power." *International Political Sociology* 5 (3): 335–39.

Cohn, Bernard S. 1996. *Colonialism and Its Forms of Knowledge: The British in India.* Princeton: Princeton University Press.

Collins, Randall. 1986. *Weberian Sociological Theory.* Cambridge: Cambridge University Press.

Connelly, Matthew James. 2008. *Fatal Misconception: The Struggle to Control World Population.* Cambridge: Harvard University Press.

Constantinou, Costas M. 2013. "Between Statecraft and Humanism: Diplomacy and Its Forms of Knowledge." *International Studies Review* 15 (2): 141–62.

Cooper, Frederick, and Randall Packard, eds. 1997. *International Development and the Social Sciences.* Berkeley: University of California Press.

Crane, Barbara B. 1993. "International Population Institutions: Adaptation to a Changing World Order." In *Institutions for the Earth: Sources of Effective International Environmental Protection*, edited by Peter M. Haas, Robert O. Keohane, and Marc A. Levy. Cambridge: MIT Press.

Critchlow, Donald. 1999. *Intended Consequences: Birth Control, Abortion, and the Federal Government in Modern America.* New York: Oxford University Press.

Cross, Maia. 2013. "Rethinking Epistemic Communities Twenty Years Later." *Review of International Studies* 39 (1): 137–60.

Cutler, Claire. 2002. "Private International Regimes and Interfirm Cooperation." In

The Emergence of Private Authority in Global Governance, edited by Thomas Bier-steker and Rodney Bruce Hall. Cambridge: Cambridge University Press.

Davis, Kingsley. 1944. "Demographic Fact and Policy in India." Paper presented at the Twenty-Second Annual Conference on the Milbank Memorial Fund, New York.

Davis, Kingsley. 1967. "Population Policies: Will Current Programs Succeed?" *Science* 158 (10): 730–39.

Demeny, Paul. 1988. "Social Science and Population Policy." *Population and Development Review* 14 (3): 451–79.

Dezalay, Yves, and Bryant G. Garth. 1996. *Dealing in Virtue: International Commercial Arbitration and the Construction of a Transnational Legal Order.* Chicago: University of Chicago Press.

Dezalay, Yves, and Bryant G. Garth. 2002. *The Internationalization of Palace Wars. Lawyers, Economists, and the Contest to Transform Latin American States.* Chicago: University of Chicago Press.

Dimitrov, Radoslav S. 2003. "Knowledge, Power, and Interests in Environmental Regime Formation." *International Studies Quarterly* 47 (1): 123–50.

Dixon-Mueller, Ruth. 1993. *Population Policy and Women's Rights: Transforming Reproductive Choice.* London: Praeger.

Dixon-Mueller, Ruth, and Adrienne Germain. 1992. "Stalking the Elusive 'Unmet Need' for Family Planning." *Studies in Family Planning* 23 (5): 330–35.

Drake, William J., and Kalypso Nicolaïdis. 1992. "Ideas, Interests, and Institutionalization: 'Trade in Services' and the Uruguay Round." *International Organization* 46 (1): 37–100.

Drezner, Daniel. 2007. *All Politics Is Global.* Princeton: Princeton University Press.

Drummond, Eric. 1931. "The Secretariat of the League of Nations." *Public Administration* 9 (2): 228–35.

Dubin, Martin David. 1983. "Transgovernmental Processes in the League of Nations." *International Organization* 37 (3): 469–93.

Dunlop, Joan. 2004. "Population and Reproductive Health: Oral History Project." In *Sophia Smith Collection,* edited by Rebecca Sharpless. Northampton MA: Smith College.

Dunlop, Joan. 2010. Personal communication, May 10.

Easterlin, Richard A. 1967. "Effects of Population Growth on the Economic Development of Developing Countries." *Annals of the American Academy of Political and Social Science* 369 (1): 98–108.

Ehrlich, Paul. 1968. *The Population Bomb.* New York: Ballantine.

Emirbayer, Mustafa. 1997. "Manifesto for a Relational Sociology." *American Journal of Sociology* 103 (2): 281–317.

Epstein, Charlotte. 2008. *The Power of Words in International Relations.* Cambridge: MIT Press.

Eriksen, Stein Sundstøl, and Ole Jacob Sending. 2013. "There Is No Global Public: The Idea of the Public and the Legitimation of Governance." *International Theory* 5 (2): 213–37.

Eriksson, Johan, and Bengt Sundelius. 2005. "Molding Minds That Form Policy: How to Make Research Useful." *International Studies Perspectives* 6 (1): 51–72.

Eyal, Gil. 2013. "Spaces between Fields." In *Bourdieu and Historical Analysis,* edited by Philips S. Gorski. Durham, NC: Duke University Press.

Feldman, Ilana. 2010. "Ad Hoc Humanity: UN Peacekeeping and the Limits of International Community in Gaza." *American Anthropologist* 112 (3): 416–29.

Finkle, Jason L., and Barbara B. Crane. 1976. "The World Health Organization and the Population Issue: Organizational Values in the United Nations." *Population and Development Review* 2 (3–4): 367–93.

Fligstein, Neil. 2002. *The Architecture of Markets: An Economic Sociology of Twenty-First-Century Capitalist Societies*. Princeton: Princeton University Press.

Fortney, Judith A. 1987. "The Importance of Family Planning in Reducing Maternal Mortality." *Studies in Family Planning* 17 (2): 109–14.

Fourcade, Marion. 2006. "The Construction of a Global Profession: The Transnationalization of Economics." *American Journal of Sociology* 112 (1): 145–94.

Fourcade, Marion. 2009. *Economists and Societies: Discipline and Profession in the United States, Britain, and France, 1890s–1990s*. Princeton: Princeton University Press.

Franck, Thomas M., and Georg Nolte. 1993. "The Good Offices Function of the UN Secretary-General." In *United Nations, Divided World*, edited by Edward Adam Roberts and Benedict Kingsbury. Oxford: Clarendon.

Fravel, Taylor. 1996. "China's Attitude toward UN Peacekeeping Operations since 1989." *Asian Survey* 36 (11): 1102–21.

Freedman, Ronald, and Lolagene Coombs. 1974. *Cross-Cultural Comparisons: Data on Two Factors in Fertility Behavior*. New York: Population Council.

Friedman, R. B. 1990. "On the Concept of Authority in Political Philosophy." In *Authority*, edited by Joseph Raz. New York: New York University Press.

Friedmann, W. G. 1952. "The United Nations and National Loyalties." *International Journal* 8 (1): 17–26.

Germain, Adrienne. 1993. "Are We Speaking the Same Language? Women's Health Advocates and Scientists Talk about Contraceptive Technology." In *Four Essays on Birth Control Needs and Risks*, edited by Ruth Dixon-Mueller and Adrienne Germain. New York: International Women's Health Coalition.

Ghosh, Amitav. 1994. "The Global Reservation: Notes toward an Ethnography of International Peacekeeping." *Cultural Anthropology* 9 (3): 412–22.

Gordon, Linda. 1974. "The Politics of Population: Birth Control and the Eugenics Movement." *Radical America* 8 (4): 66–69.

Gorski, Philip S., ed. 2013. *Bourdieu and Historical Analysis*. Durham: Duke University Press.

Gorski, Philip S. 2013. "Conclusion: Bourdieusian theory and historical analysis: Maps, Mechanisms, and Methods." In *Bourdieu and Historical Analysis*, edited by Philip S. Gorski, 327–66. Durham: Duke University Press.

Greenhalgh, Susan. 1996. "The Social Construction of Population Science: An Intellectual, Institutional, and Political History of Twentieth Century Demography." *Comparative Study of Society and History* 38 (1): 22–66.

Greenhalgh, Susan. 2012. "On the Crafting of Population Knowledge." *Population and Development Review* 38 (1): 121–31.

Greenhill, Brian. 2008. "Recognition and Collective Identity Formation in International Politics." *European Journal of International Relations* 14 (2): 343–68.

Grepp, Roy O., M. A. Koblisky, and F. S. Jaffe. 1976. *Reproduction and Human Welfare:*

A Challenge to Research: A Review of the Reproductive Sciences and Contraceptive Development. Cambridge: MIT Press.

Guzzini, Stefano. 2000. "A Reconstruction of Constructivism in International Relations Theory." *European Journal of International Relations* 6 (2): 147–82.

Guzzini, Stefano. 2013. "Power." In *Bourdieu in International Relations: Rethinking Key Concepts in IR*, edited by Rebecca Adler-Nissen. London: Routledge.

Haas, Peter M. 1992. "Epistemic Communities and International Policy." *International Organization* 46 (1): 1–35.

Halfon, Saul. 2000. "Reconstructing Population Policy after Cairo: Demography, Women's Empowerment, and the Population Network." PhD diss., Cornell University.

Hall, Rodney Bruce, and Thomas Biersteker. 2002. *The Emergence of Private Authority in Global Governance.* Cambridge: Cambridge University Press.

Hammarskjöld, Dag. 1960. *Official Records of the 883rd Meeting, 3 October, 1960.* New York: UN General Assembly.

Hammarskjöld, Dag. 1961. *The International Civil Servant in Law and in Fact: A Lecture Delivered to Congregation on 30 May 1961.* Oxford: Clarendon.

Hansen, Lene. 2006. *Security as Practice: Discourse Analysis and the Bosnian war.* New York: Routledge.

Hardin, Garrett. 1968. "The Tragedy of the Commons." *Science* 162: 1243–48.

Harkavy, Oscar. 1995. *Curbing Population Growth: An Insider's Perspective on the Population Movement.* New York: Springer.

Hauser, Phillip M. 1969. "Non-Family Planning Methods of Population Control." Paper presented at Pakistan International Family Planning Conference, Dacca.

Higer, Amy J. 1997. "Transnational Movements and World Politics: The International Women's Health Movement and Population Policy." PhD diss., Brandeis University.

Hill, Reuben. 1968. "A Classified International Bibliography of Family Planning Research, 1955–1968." *Demography* 5 (2): 973–1001.

Hindess, Barry. 2004. "Liberalism: What's in a Name?" In *Global Governmentality: Governing International Spaces,* edited by Wendy Larner and William Walters. London: Routledge.

Hodgson, Dennis. 1988. "Orthodoxy and Revisionism in American Demography." *Population and Development Review* 14 (4): 541–69.

Hodgson, Dennis. 1991. "The Ideological Origins of the Population Association of America." *Population and Development Review* 17 (1): 1–34.

Hodgson, Dennis, and Susan Cotts Watkins. 1997. "Feminists and Neo-Malthusians: Past and Present Alliances." *Population and Development Review* 23 (3): 469–523.

Holland, Ben. 2010. "Sovereignty as Dominium? Reconstructing the Constructivist Roman Law Thesis." *International Studies Quarterly* 54 (2): 449–80.

Honneth, Axel. 1995. *The Struggle for Recognition: The Moral Grammar of Social Conflict.* Cambridge: Polity.

Hopgood, Stephen. 2006. *Keepers of the Flame: Inside Amnesty International.* Ithaca: Cornell University Press.

Hopgood, Stephen. 2009. "Moral Authority, Modernity and the Politics of the Sacred." *European Journal of International Relations* 15 (2): 229–55.

Hurd, Ian. 1999. "Legitimacy and Authority in International Politics." *International Organization* 53 (2): 379–408.

Hurd, Ian. 2005. "The Strategic Use of Liberal Internationalism: Libya and the UN Sanctions, 1992–2003." *International Organization* 59 (3): 495–526.

Ingold, Tim. 2000. *The Perception of the Environment: Essays on Livelihood, Dwelling, and Skill.* London: Routledge.

International Civil Service Commission. 2013. *Standards of Conduct for the International Civil Service.* New York: United Nations. Available at http://www.un.org/en/ethics/pdf/StandConIntCivSE.pdf.

International Women's Health Coalition and Cidadania, Estudos, Pesquisa, Informação, Ação. 1994. *Reproductive Health and Justice—International Women's Health Conference for Cairo '94.* New York: International Women's Health Coalition, ; Rio de Janeiro: Cidadania, Estudos, Pesquisa, Informação, Ação.

Jacobson, Harold K. 1962. "The United Nations and Colonialism: A Tentative Appraisal." *International Organization* 16 (11): 37–56.

Jabri, Vivienne. 2013. "Peacebuilding, the Local and the International: A Colonial or a Postcolonial Rationality?" *Peacebuilding* 1 (1): 3–16.

Jain, Anrudh, Judith Bruce, and Barbara Mensch. 1992. "Setting Standards of Quality in Family Planning Programs." *Studies in Family Planning* 23 (6): 392–95.

Joyner, Christopher. 2002. "The United Nations: Strengthening an International Norm." In *Exporting Democracy: Rhetoric vs. Reality,* edited by Peter Schraeder. Boulder, CO: Rienner.

Kahler, Miles, and David Lake, eds. 2003. *Governance in a Global Economy: Political Authority in Transition.* Princeton: Princeton University Press.

Kay, David A. 1966. "Secondment in the United Nations Secretariat: An Alternative View." *International Organization* 20 (1): 63–75.

Keck, Margaret, and Kathryn Sikkink. 1998. *Activists beyond Borders.* Ithaca: Cornell University Press.

Kennedy, David. 1986. "The Move to Institutions." *Cardozo Law Review* 8 (5): 841–988.

Keohane, Robert O. 1984. *After Hegemony: Cooperation and Discord in the World Political Economy.* Princeton: Princeton University Press.

Keohane, Robert O., and Lisa L. Martin. 1995. "The Promise of Institutionalist Theory." *International Security* 20 (1): 39–51.

Kevles, Daniel. 1985. *In the Name of Eugenics: Genetics and the Uses of Human Heredity.* New York: Knopf.

Kirk, Dudley. 1964. Memo to Frank Notestein, "Comments on Priorities in National Family Planning Programs," January 22, 1964. Population Council Subject File, Rockefeller Archive Center, Sleepy Hollow, NY.

Kiser, Clyde. 1971. "The Work of the Milbank Memorial Fund in Population since 1928." *Milbank Memorial Fund Quarterly* 49 (4, pt. 2): 15–62.

Kissinger, Henry. 1994. *Diplomacy.* New York: Simon and Schuster.

Koremenos, Barbara, Charles Lipson, and Duncan Snidal. 2001. "The Rational Design of International Institutions." *International Organization* 55 (4): 761–99.

Koskenniemi, Martti. 2002. *The Gentle Civilizer of Nations: The Rise and Fall of International Law, 1870–1960.* Cambridge: Cambridge University Press.

Krasner, Stephen D. 2004. "Sharing Sovereignty: New Institutions for Collapsed and Failing States." *International Security* 29 (2): 85–120.

Kratochwill, Friedrich. 2014. *The Status of Law in World Society: Meditations on the Role and Rule of Law*. Cambridge: Cambridge University Press.

Krebs, Ronald R., and Patrick Thaddeus Jackson. 2007. "Twisting Tongues and Twisting Arms: The Power of Political Rhetoric." *European Journal of International Relations* 13 (1): 35–66.

Krois, Jon Michael. 1987. *Cassirer: Symbolic Forms and History*. New Haven: Yale University Press.

Kuznets, Simon. 1967. "Population and Economic Growth." Paper presented at Proceeding of the American Philosophical Society.

Lake, David. 2009. *Hierarchy in International Relations*. Ithaca: Cornell University Press.

Lake, David. 2010. "Rightful Rules: Authority, Order, and the Foundations of Global Governance." *International Studies Quarterly* 54 (3): 587–613.

Leira, Halvard. 2011. "The Emergence of Foreign Policy: Knowledge, Discourse, History." PhD diss., University of Oslo.

Lengyel, Peter. 1959. "Some Trends in the International Civil Service." *International Organization* 13 (4): 520–37.

Lindemann, Thomas. 2010. *Causes of War: The Struggle for Recognition*. Colchester: ECPR.

Litfin, Karen. 1994. *Ozone Discourses: Science and Politics in Global Environmental Cooperation*. New York: Columbia University Press.

Lorimer, Frank, and Frederick Osborn. 1934. *Dynamics of Population: Social and Biological Significance of the Changing Birth Rates in the United States*. New York: Macmillan.

MacFarlane, S. Neil, and Albrecht Schnabel. 1995. "Russia's Approach to Peacekeeping." *International Journal* 50 (2): 294–324.

MacMillan, Margaret. 2007. *Paris 1919: Six Months That Changed the World*. New York: Random House.

Madsen, Mikael Rask. 2011. "Reflexivity and the Construction of the International Object: The case of Human Rights." *International Political Sociology* 5 (3): 259–75.

Mahler, Halfdan. 1979. "Rescue Mission for Tomorrow's Health: Interview with Dr. Halfdan Mahler." *People* 6 (2): 25–28.

Mamdani, Mahmoud. 1972. *The Myth of Population Control*. New York: Monthly Review Press.

March, James G., and Johan P. Olsen. 1998. "The Institutional Dynamics of International Political Orders." *International Organization* 52 (44): 943–69.

Markell, Patchen. 2003. *Bound by Recognition*. Princeton: Princeton University Press.

Martin, John Levi. 2003. "What Is Field Theory?" *American Journal of Sociology*, 109 (1): 1–49.

Mauldin, W. Parker. 1965. "Fertility Studies: Knowledge, Attitude, Practice." *Studies in Family Planning* 1 (7): 1–10.

McAdam, Doug, Sidney Tarrow, and Charles Tilly. 2001. *Dynamics of Contention*. Cambridge: Cambridge University Press.

McCann, Carolyn. 1994. *Birth Control Politics in America, 1916–1945*. Ithaca: Cornell University Press.

McLean, Donald. 1952a. "Memo, from McLean" June 23, 1952. JDR III Papers, Series 1, Subseries 5, Box 81, Folder 674. New York: Rockefeller Archive Center.

McLean, Donald. 1952b. "Miscellaneous Notes on Population Conference." JDR III Papers, Series 1, Subseries 5, Box 81, Folder 674. New York: Rockefeller Archive Center.

McLean, Donald. 1952c. "Record of Meeting January 20th 1952 with McLean, Strauss, Notestein and Parran." JDR III papers, Series 1, Subseries 5, Box 81, Folder 674. New York: Rockefeller Archive Center.

Mehta, Uday Singh. 1999. *Liberalism and Empire: A Study in Nineteenth Century British Liberal Thought*. Chicago: University of Chicago Press.

Mitchell, Timothy. 1991. "The Limits of the State: Beyond Statist Approaches and Their Critics." *American Political Science Review* 85 (1): 77–96.

Moore, H. E. 1954. *The Population Bomb*. New York: Hugh Moore Fund.

Mösslang, Markus, and Torsten Riotte. 2008. *The Diplomats' World: A Cultural History of Diplomacy, 1815–1914*. New York: Oxford University Press.

Neumann, Iver B. 2013. *Diplomatic Sites*. New York: Columbia University Press.

Neumann, Iver B., and Ole Jacob Sending. 2010. *Governing the Global Polity*. Ann Arbor: University of Michigan Press.

Notestein, Frank W. 1944. "Problems of Policy in Relation to Areas of Heavy Population Pressure." *Milbank Memorial Fund Quarterly* 22 (4): 424–44.

Notestein, Frank W. 1945. "Population–The Long View." In *Food for the World*, edited by Theodore W. Schultz. Chicago: University of Chicago Press.

Notestein, Frank W. 1947. "Summary of the Demographic Background of Problems of Underdeveloped Areas." *Milbank Memorial Fund Quarterly* 26 (3): 249–55.

Notestein, Frank W. 1950. "The Reduction of Human Fertility as an Aid to Programs of Economic Development in Densely Settled Agrarian Regions." In *1949 Annual Conference of the Milbank Memorial Fund*. New York: Milbank Memorial Fund.

Notestein, Frank W. 1961. "Letter from Frank Notestein to Dana Creel, the Rockefeller Brothers Fund, Sept. 22, 1961" IV3B4.2 Box 4, "Demographic Division 1957–1966," Folder 41. New York: Rockefeller Archive Center.

Notestein, Frank W. 1968. "The Population Council and the Demographic Crisis of the Less Developed World." *Demography* 5 (2): 553–60.

Notestein, Frank W. 1982. "Demography in the United States: A Partial Account of the Development of the Field." *Population and Development Review* 8 (4): 651–87.

Nye, Joseph S., and Robert O. Keohane. 1971. "Transnational Relations and World Politics: An Introduction." *International Organization* 25 (3): 329–49.

Omran, Abdel R. 1987. *Interrelations between Maternal and Neo-Natal Health and Family Planning: Conceptualization of the Theme*. New York: Plenum.

Omran, Abdel R., C. C. Standley, and Joseph E. Azar. 1976. *Family Formation Patterns and Health: An International Collaborative Study in India, Iran, Lebanon, Philippines, and Turkey*. Geneva: World Health Organization.

Onuf, Nicholas, and Frank F. Klink. 1989. "Anarchy, Authority, Rule." *International Studies Quarterly* 33 (2): 149–73.

Openheim, L. 1919. *The League of Nations and Its Problems—In Three Lectures.* London: Longmans, Green.

Orford, Anne. 2011. *International Authority and the Responsibility to Protect.* Cambridge: Cambridge University Press.

Osborn, Fairfield. 1948/1968. *Our Plundered Planet.* New York: Pyramid.

Oudshoorn, Nelly. 1997. "From Population Control Politics to Chemicals: The WHO as an Intermediary Organization in Contraceptive Development." *Social Studies of Science* 27 (1): 41–72.

Paris, Roland. 2004. *At War's End: Building Peace after Civil Conflict.* Cambridge: Cambridge University Press.

Pedersen, Susan. 2007. "Back to the League of Nations." *The American Historical Review.* 112 (4): 1091–1117.

Phelan, Edward J. 1933. "The New International Civil Service." *Foreign Affairs* 11 (January): 307–14.

Population Council. 1953. Agenda for Discussion of Program, April 20, 1953. In Rockefeller Family Archives, Rockefeller Archive Center, Sleepy Hollow, NY.

Population Council. 1974. *Annual Report.* New York: Population Council.

Population Council. 1976. *Annual Report.* New York: Population Council.

Population Council. 1977. *Annual Report.* New York: Population Council.

Population Council. 1987. *Better Health for Women and Children through Family Planning.* New York: Population Council.

Potter, Pitman B. 1931. "Permanent Delegations to the League of Nations." *American Political Science Review* 25 (1): 21–44.

Pouliot, Vincent. 2007. "'Subjectivism': Toward a Constructivist Methodology." *International Studies Quarterly* 51 (2): 359–84.

Price, Richard M. 2003. "Transnational Civil Society and Advocacy in World Politics." *World Politics* 55 (4): 579–606.

Ramcharan, B. G. 1982. "The Good Offices of the United Nations Secretary-General in the Field of Human Rights." *American Journal of International Law* 76 (1): 130–41.

Ranshofen-Wertheimer, Egon Ferdinand. 1945. *The Position of the Executive and Administrative Heads of the United Nations International Organizations.* Washington, DC: Carnegie Endowment for International Peace.

Rathbun, B. C. 2012. *Trust in International Cooperation: The Creation of International Security Institutions and the Domestic Politics of American Multilateralism.* Cambridge: Cambridge University Press.

Raulet, Harry M. 1970. "Family Planning and Population Control in Developing Countries." *Demography* 7 (2): 211–34.

Rawls, John. 1999. *A Theory of Justice.* Rev. ed. Cambridge: Harvard University Press.

Reed, James. 1978. *From Private Vice to Public Virtue. The Birth Control Movement and American Society since 1830.* New York: Basic Books.

Reus-Smit, Christian. 1999. *The Moral Purpose of the State: Culture, Social Identity, and Institutional Rationality in International Relations.* Princeton: Princeton University Press.

Risse, Thomas. 2012. "Transnational Actors in World Politics." In *Handbook of International Relations,* edited by Walter Carlsnaes, Thomas Risse, and Beth Simmons. London: Sage.

Risse, Thomas, Stephen C. Ropp, and Kathryn Sikkink, eds. 1999. *The Power of Human Rights: International Norms and Domestic Change.* Cambridge: Cambridge University Press.

Robinson, Pearl T. 2008. "Ralph Bunche and African Studies: Reflections on the Politics of Knowledge." *African Studies Review* 51 (1): 1–16.

Rockefeller Archive Center. 1963. Population Subject File. Sleepy Hollow, NY.

Rockefeller Archive Center. 1964. "Conference on Strategy for Implementing Family Planning in Developing Countries," Summary, New York, USA. January 24–25, 1964. Record Group IV3B4.6/Population Council Subject File, Box 122, Folder 2236. Sleepy Hollow, NY.

Rockefeller Archive Center. 1965. "Minutes of meeting at the Population Council October 5–7, 1965," Population Subject File, Record Group IVB4.6, Box 128, Folder 2364. Sleepy Hollow, NY.

Rockefeller, John D., III. 1974. "Population Growth: The Role of the Developed World." *Population and Development Review* 4 (3): 509–16.

Rosenau, James. 1992. "Governance, Order, and Change in World Politics." In *Governance without Government: Order and Change in World Politics,* edited by James Rosenau and Ernst-Otto Czempiel. Cambridge: Cambridge University Press.

Rosenau, James. 1999. "Toward an Ontology for Global Governance." In *Approaches to Global Governance Theory,* edited by Martin Hewson and Timothy J. Sinclair. New York: New York State University Press.

Rosenfield, Allan G. 1976. "Family Planning Programs: Can More Be Done?" *Studies in Family Planning* 5 (4): 115–22.

Ross, Dorothy. 1991. *The Origins of American Social Science.* New York: Cambridge University Press.

Ross, Edward A. 1927. *Standing Room Only.* London: Century.

Sacriste, Guillaume, and Antoine Vauchez. 2007. "The Force of International Law: Lawyers' Diplomacy on the International Scene in the 1920s." *Law and Social Inquiry* 32 (1): 83–107.

Sassen, Saskia. 2007. "Global: An Expanded Analytic Terrain." In *Globalization Theory: Approaches and Controversies,* edited by David Held and Anthony McGrew. Cambridge: Polity.

Schachter, Oscar. 1962. "Dag Hammarskjöld and the Relation of Law to Politics." *American Journal of International Law* 56 (1): 1–8.

Schia, Niels Nagelhus. 2015. *Peacebuilding, Ownership, and Sovereignty from New York to Monrovia: A Multi-Sited Ethnographic Approach.* PhD Dissertation, Department of Anthropology. Oslo: University of Oslo.

Schiff, Jade. 2014. *Burdens of Political Responsibility: Narrative, Ontology, Responsiveness.* Cambridge: Cambridge University Press.

Schultz, Theodore W. 1945. Introduction to *Food for the World,* edited by Theodore W. Schultz. Chicago: University of Chicago Press.

Schwebel, Stephen M. 1994. *Justice in International Law: Selected Writings.* Cambridge: Cambridge University Press.

Seabrooke, Leonard. 2006. *The Social Sources of Financial Power: Domestic Legitimacy and International Financial Orders.* Ithaca: Cornell University Press.

Seabrooke, Leonard. 2014. "Epistemic Arbitrage: Transnational Professional Knowledge in Action." *Journal of Professions and Organisation* 1 (1): 49–64.

Seabrooke, Leonard, and Eleni Tsingou. 2009. *Revolving Doors and Linked Ecologies in the World Economy: Policy Locations and the Practice of International Financial Reform.* Coventry: University of Warwick, Centre for the Study of Globalisation and Regionalisation.

Sending, Ole Jacob. 2009. "Why Peacebuilders Fail to Secure Ownership and Be Sensitive to Context." In *Security in Practice.* Oslo: NUPI.

Sending, Ole Jacob. 2011. "United by Difference: Diplomacy as a Thin Culture." *International Journal* 66 (3): 643–59.

Sending, Ole Jacob, Vincent Pouliot, and Iver B. Neumann. 2014. Introduction to *Diplomacy and the Making of World Politics*, ed. Ole Jacob Sending, Vincent Pouliot, and Iver B. Neumann. Cambridge: Cambridge University Press.

Sharp, Paul. 2009. *Diplomatic Theory of International Relations.* Cambridge: Cambridge University Press.

Sharp, Paul, and Geoffrey Wiseman. 2007. *The Diplomatic Corps as an Institution of International Society.* Basingstoke: Palgrave Macmillan.

Sikkink, Kathryn. 2002. "Restructuring World Politics: The Limits and Asymmetries of Soft Power." In *Restructuring World Politics: Transnational Social Movements, Networks, and Norms*, edited by S. Khagram, J. V. Riker, and K. Sikkink. Minneapolis: University of Minnesota Press.

Simon, Julian. 1977. *The Economics of Population Growth.* Princeton: Princeton University Press.

Simon, Julian. 1981. *The Ultimate Resources.* Princeton: Princeton University Press.

Simpson, Gerry. 2001. "Two Liberalisms." *European Journal of International Law* 12 (3): 537–72.

Sinding, Steven W. 2000. "The Great Population Debates: How Relevant Are They for the 21st Century?" *American Journal of Public Health* 90 (12): 1841–45.

Sinding, Steven W., John A. Ross, and Allan G. Rosenfield. 1994. "Seeking Common Ground: Unmet Need and Demographic Goals." *International Family Planning Perspectives* 20 (1): 23–27, 32.

Sofer, Sasson. 1997. "The Diplomat as a Stranger." *Diplomacy and Statecraft* 8 (3): 179–86.

Steiner, Zara S. 1969. *The Foreign Office and Foreign Policy, 1898–1914.* London: Cambridge University Press.

Steinmetz, George. 2006. "Bourdieu's Disavowal of Lacan." *Constellations* 13 (4): 445–64.

Steinmetz, George. 2008a. "The Colonial State as a Social Field: Ethnographic Capital and Native Policy in the German Overseas Empire before 1914." *American Review of Sociology* 73 (4): 589–612.

Steinmetz, George. 2008b. *The Devil's Handwriting: Precoloniality and the German Colonial State in Qingdao, Samoa, and Southwest Africa.* Chicago: University of Chicago Press.

Stycos, Mayone J. 1964. "Survey Research and Population Control in Latin America." *Public Opinion Quarterly* 28 (3): 367–72.

Swidler, Ann. 2009. "Dialectics of Patronage." In *Globalization, Philanthropy, and*

Civil Society: Projecting Institutional Logics Abroad, edited by David Hammack and Steven Heydemann. Bloomington: Indiana University Press.

Symonds, Richard, and Michael Carder. 1973. *The United Nations and the Population Question, 1945–1970*. London: Chatto and Windus for Sussex University Press.

Szreter, Simon. 1993. "The Idea of Demographic Transition and the Study of Fertility Change." *Population and Development Review* 34 (4): 659–701.

Szreter, Simon. 1996. *Fertility, Class, and Gender in Britain, 1860–1940*. Cambridge: Cambridge University Press.

Thant Myint-U and Amy Scott. 2007. *The UN Secretariat: A Brief History*. New York: International Peace Academy.

Toulmin, Stephen. 1992. *Cosmopolis: The Hidden Agenda of Modernity*. Chicago: University of Chicago Press.

UN. 1960. *Official Records of the 869th Meeting, 23 September 1960*. New York: UN General Assembly.

UN. 1992. "An Agenda for Peace: Preventive Diplomacy, Peacemaking, and Peace-Keeping." In *Report of the Secretary General*. New York: United Nations.

UN. 1995. *Programme of Action Adopted at the International Conference on Population and Development, Cairo*. New York: UN.

UN. 2004. *Report of the International Civil Service Commission for 2004*. New York: General Assembly Official Records.

UN. 2006. *Tenth Progress Report of the Secretary-General on the United Nations Mission in Liberia*. New York: United Nations Security Council.

UN. 2008. *Working Group on Lessons Learned Special Session, 12 June 2008*. New York: United Nations Peacebuilding Commission.

UN. 2009. *Report of the Secretary-General on Peacebuilding in the Immediate Aftermath of Conflict*. New York: United Nations.

UN. 2011. *Twenty-Second Progress Report of the Secretary-General on the United Nations Mission in Liberia*. New York: United Nations Security Council.

UN Office of the High Commissioner on Human Rights. 2006. *Rule-of-Law Tools for Post-Conflict States: An Operational Framework*. New York: United Nations.

United States. 1984. "US Policy Statement for the International Conference on Population." *Population and Development Review* 10 (3): 574–79.

Urquhart, Brian. 1993. *Ralph Bunche: An American Life*. New York: W. W. Norton.

Vauchez, Antoine. 2011. "Interstitial Power in Fields of Limited Statehood: Introducing a 'Weak Field' Approach to the Study of Transnational Settings." *International Political Sociology* 5 (3): 340–45.

Vogt, William. 1948. *Road to Survival*. New York: Sloane.

Volberda, Henk W., and Arie Y. Lewin. 2003. "Co-Evolutionary Dynamics within and between Firms: From Evolution to Co-Evolution." *Journal of Management Studies* 40 (8): 2111–36.

Wacquant, Loïc. 2005b. "Symbolic Power in the Rule of the 'State Nobility.'" In *Pierre Bourdieu and Democratic Politics: The Mystery of Ministry*, edited by Loïc Wacquant. Cambridge: Polity.

Wagner, Peter. 1994. *A Sociology of Modernity Liberty and Discipline*. London: Routledge.

Wagner, Peter. 2001. *A History and Theory of the Social Sciences: Not All That Is Solid Melts into Air.* London: Sage.

Wagner, Peter, Bjørn Wittrock, and Richard Whitley. 1991. *Discourses on Society: The Shaping of the Social Science Disciplines.* Dordrecht: Kluwer Academic.

Warwick, Donald P. 1983. "The KAP Survey: Dictates of Mission versus Demands of Science." In *Social Research in Developing Countries: Surveys and Censuses in the Third World,* edited by Martin Bulmer and Donald P. Warwick. Chichester: Wiley.

Warwick, Donald P. 1994. "Politics of Research on Fertility Control." *Population and Development Review* 20 (Sup.): 179–93.

Weaver, Catherine. 2008. *Hypocrisy Trap: The World Bank and Poverty Reform.* Princeton: Princeton University Press.

Weber, Max. 1978. *Economy and Society.* Berkeley: University of California Press.

Wendt, Alexander. 2003. "Why a World State Is Inevitable." *European Journal of International Relations* 9 (4): 491–542.

Wertheim, Stephen. 2012. "The League of Nations: A Retreat from International Law?" *Journal of Global History* 7 (2): 210–32.

Whelpton, Pascal K. 1954. "Research Needs and Suggested Projects." Paper presented at the Annual Conference of the Milbank Memorial Fund, New York.

Whitney, Vincent Heath. 1976. "Population Planning in Asia in the 1970s." *Population Studies* 30 (2): 337–51.

WHO. 1980. *The Work of WHO, 1978–1979: Biennial Report of the Director-General to the World Health Assembly and to the United Nations.* Geneva: WHO.

WHO. 1982. *The Work of WHO, 1980–1981: Biennial Report of the Director-General to the World Health Assembly and to the United Nations.* Geneva: WHO.

WHO. 1986. *The Work of WHO, 1984–1985: Biennial Report of the Director-General to the World Health Assembly and to the United Nations.* Geneva: WHO.

WHO. 1994. "Challenges in Reproductive Health Research: Biennial Report, 1992–1993." In *Development and Research Training in Human Reproduction,* edited by J. Khanna, P. F. A, Van Look, and P. D. Griffin. Geneva: UNDP/UNFPA/WHO/World Bank.

Wiehl, Dorothy. 1971. "Discussions." In *Forty Years of Research in Human Fertility: Retrospect and Prospect,* edited by Clyde Kiser. New York: Milbank Memorial Fund.

Williams, Michael C. 2012. "Culture." In *Bourdieu in International Relations: Rethinking Key Concepts in IR,* edited by Rebecca Adler-Nissen. London: Routledge.

Winchmore, Charles. 1965. "The Secretariat: Retrospect and Prospect." *International Organization* 19 (3): 622–39.

Wolfson, Margaret. 1983. *Profiles in Population Assistance—A Comparative Review of the Principal Donor Agencies.* Paris: OECD Development Centre.

Zeidenstein, George. 1977. "Strategic Issues in Population." *Population and Development Review* 3 (3): 307–18.

Zürn, Michael, Martin Binder, and Matthias Ecker-Ehrhardt. 2012. "International Authority and Its Politicization." *International Theory* 4 (1): 69–106.

Index